Have You Heard the News?

In Pensacola, Florida, a religious spectacle is under way.
Night after night, people from all over the world come
by the thousands hoping for a divine encounter.
BARBARA WALTERS, ABC NEWS, "20/20"

[Stephen Hill is] white-hot, the charismatic center of a whole
culture's attention. From bell to bell, he has his listeners
by the scruff of the neck . . . You have never in your life
experienced religion so fulfilling, total and joyful.
MARK SCHONE, *SPIN MAGAZINE*

[The Brownsville Revival] has become the epicenter for
the Pentecostal revival movement. A booming, big-time,
fire-and-brimstone-driven, nightly event.
RUSS JAMISON, CNN "HEADLINE NEWS"

This is Christ as The Terminator, taking names and kicking souls,
letting only those who have embraced Him enter into Heaven.
DEBORAH SHARP, *USA TODAY*

[Stephen Hill is] a barrel-chested evangelist
with the charisma of a rock star.
DEBORAH KOVACH CALDWELL,
THE DALLAS MORNING NEWS

His voice was as a trumpet and his words were as fire
and the people were filled with the spirit of holiness.
PETER CARLSON, *THE WASHINGTON POST*

This is no-nonsense religion where the way to salvation
takes devotion and dedication . . . It's that
"old time religion"—with a newfound fervor.
"FOX 10 NEWS"

Pensacola, Florida—the end of the earth, by
biblical standards, but the very center of the universe
if you're looking to experience the Holy Spirit.
BETH DICKEY, "THE POWER OF THE HOLY SPIRIT"
NEWSWEEK

[Stephen Hill] reaches for the bleakest sinner with
one hand even as he gropes for the comfortable,
social-club Christian with the other.
Both, he warns, will bust hell wide open.
RICK BRAGG, *THE NEW YORK TIMES*

The Spirit will move you, but it's not rock and roll.
This is an old fashioned revival—some say
the biggest in over 100 years.
NBC NEWS, "THE TODAY SHOW"

The service shifts into high gear after the sermon,
when evangelist [Stephen] Hill delivers his urgent call to the altar.
It sends sinners running, a countdown to salvation . . .
Clearly, this is not church as usual.
LYNN SHERR, ABC NEWS, "20/20"

The reverend Stephen Hill [is] a fire-breathing evangelist.
"HARD COPY"

Now that he's the successful person that he always
imagined in his boyhood dreams, [Stephen Hill] wants to tell
you how his life used to swirl like the spin cycle on a
washing machine, twisting him into tight, wrung-out knots.
He wants to tell you that he dealt drugs out of a
U-Totem convenience store, where he worked as a cashier.
He wants to tell you that he broke into veterinarians' offices
and stole the needles and the tranquilizers because he wanted
to find out if animals got a better buzz.
He wants to tell it all, don't you know, because the foot-
stompers who pack the brown-brick church down in Pensacola
are yearning to know this: If God can save such a terrible
teenager as Stephen Hill—someone who popped pills and
dropped LSD—He can save you, too.
MIKE MARSHALL, *THE HUNTSVILLE TIMES*

Today, [Stephen] Hill tells the thousands who flock to Brownsville
that in a fallen world, only Jesus sets man free . . . Muslims and Jews
have converted at the altar. A Buddhist woman declared that
Buddha never did anything for her the way Jesus did. Gang leaders,
drug addicts and dealers have come forward. And the abuser and
the abused have wept before an equally teary congregation.
LISA SINGH, *THE RICHMOND TIMES-DISPATCH*

People from all walks of life have come to the altar at the
Brownsville Assembly of God . . . Drug addicts, prostitutes, business-
men, homosexuals and more have all found new life in Christ.
LEE WEBB, CBN

KNOCKIN' AT HEAVEN'S DOOR

STEPHEN HILL

KNOCKIN' AT HEAVEN'S DOOR

STEPHEN HILL

Regal

A Division of Gospel Light
Ventura, California, U.S.A.

Published by Regal Books
A Division of Gospel Light
Ventura, California, U.S.A.
Printed in U.S.A.

Regal Books is a ministry of Gospel Light, an evangelical Christian publisher dedicated to serving the local church. We believe God's vision for Gospel Light is to provide church leaders with biblical, user-friendly materials that will help them evangelize, disciple and minister to children, youth and families.

It is our prayer that this Regal book will help you discover biblical truth for your own life and help you meet the needs of others. May God richly bless you.

For a free catalog of resources from Regal Books/Gospel Light please call your Christian supplier, or contact us at 1-800-4-GOSPEL or at www.gospellight.com.

The names of certain individuals mentioned have been changed
to protect their privacy and to maintain confidentiality.

Published in association with the literary agency of Alive Communications, Inc., 1465 Kelly Johnson Blvd., Suite 320, Colorado Springs, Colorado 80920.

Cover Design by Kevin Keller
Interior Design by Britt Rocchio
Edited by Deena Davis

Library of Congress Cataloging-in-Publication Data
Hill, Stephen, 1954-
Knockin' at heaven's door / Stephen Hill.
    p.   cm.
Includes bibliographical references.
ISBN 0-8307-2498-2 (Hardcover)
ISBN 0-8307-2493-1 (Trade paperback)
1. Christian life.   I. Title.
BV4501.2.H457   1999   99-23011
243–DC21   CIP

1 2 3 4 5 6 7 8 9 10 11 12 13 14 15 16 17 / 05 04 03 02 01 00 99

Rights for publishing this book in other languages are contracted by Gospel Literature International (GLINT). GLINT also provides technical help for the adaptation, translation and publishing of Bible study resources and books in scores of languages worldwide. For further information, write to GLINT, P.O. Box 4060, Ontario, CA 91761-1003, U.S.A. You may also send E-mail to Glintint@aol.com, or visit their website at www.glint.org.

ACKNOWLEDGMENTS

I've always loved teamwork. The book you hold in your hands has been burning in my heart for the last 12 months. With my intense schedule, it would never have come to completion without the aid of other vital contributors. It is my honor to recognize them.

First of all, special thanks to Steve Rabey for adding so much to this book. Much of what you will read in these pages is actually written and transcribed sermons that Steve helped me organize and arrange into a cohesive whole.

Without the research efforts of three people, this book would have lacked the rubber-meets-the-road quality of newsworthy statistics and real-people stories. My profound appreciation goes to my brother, George Hill, who tracked down sources, researched websites, and kept me up to date with breaking world news. Warm thanks to Tomi Kaiser and Douglas Hawks, who compiled research and made it easier for me to sift through and select information for inclusion in this book.

Also, please allow me to acknowledge the dedicated help of Veronica Rosas and Becky Rogers for helping me polish and buff the final manuscript.

Thanks, team, for your consistent labor and zeal in this project. Without you, *Knockin' at Heaven's Door* would not be a reality.

CONTENTS

TO THE READER

Every year, there are between 50,000 and 60,000 books published in America. These books are written for many different reasons. Some are novels, designed to entertain. Others are serious books about history or science. Still others are written for money and money alone. In these cases, both the writer and the publisher seize the opportunity to rake in the cash.

I have written this book you now hold in your hands out of obedience. I feel a mandate from heaven to pen the words that God has spoken to my heart. There is an urgency in my soul. I cannot be quiet.

I'm not after big sales or popularity. The majority doesn't rule when it comes to truth. My responsibility ends with the completion of this book. Outside of my personal prayer for you, my work is done now. The rest is up to you.

Since June 1995, I have been preaching at revival services at a church in the small Gulf Coast city of Pensacola, Florida.

Why have more than three million people from all walks of life, every denomination, and every corner of the globe attended these revival meetings? Why do thousands of God-hungry souls fill coliseums to attend the Awake America crusades that we hold across the nation? Why is there such an overwhelming response to the repentance message when these crusade services are carried live on television in several major cities?

Why? The answer, my friend, is quite simple. They're tired of lukewarm, watered-down messages from the pulpit. They want to hear an uncompromising message about getting right with God.

Night after night, when it's time to preach, the following simple five-point message is emphasized. This message is the heartbeat of the revival, and it is one that the majority of North Americans believe to be true:

1. We are all sinners. (And sin, by the way, is anything Jesus wouldn't do.)
2. Sin separates us from God.
3. God provided a remedy for our lost, sinful condition through the sacrifice of His Son, Jesus Christ.
4. If you will believe in Jesus, repent of your sin and confess Him as Lord, you will be saved.
5. Once you become a Christian, you leave your sinful lifestyle behind.

This book is not for everyone. It is strictly for those who want to know God and are willing to do what it takes to please Him. The bottom line is this: Regardless of your present spiritual condition, God can touch you if you're willing. Not only will He touch you, He'll open up heaven to you.

When we love Jesus and obey His will for our lives, the door of heaven will be opened. Then we will truly know the love, peace and joy of Christ. That's what this book is about. I pray that God will use it to speak to your life. Whether you're young or old, rich or poor, I want you to experience what it means to live under an open heaven here on earth. And, my friend, when your life is over, you won't find yourself knockin' at heaven's door...it will be swung wide open.

Sincerely,

1

KNOCKIN' AT HEAVEN'S DOOR

Just about everybody believes in heaven.
Do you?
Do you know what it takes to get there, and how to
experience the reality of heaven now?

Life hasn't been the same for me since Father's Day, 1995. On that Sunday morning, while I was preaching at the Brownsville Assembly of God in Pensacola, Florida, the power of God came upon us in an amazing way. Ever since, I've been preaching at Brownsville revival meetings that can stretch on past midnight.

Revival has changed the church, and it has altered the lives of everyone who has been involved in it. Heaven has truly been opened over this church.

For me, and for the millions of people who have visited the revival, heaven isn't something remote or far away. Of course, heaven *is* a literal place, but it's much more than that. And it's not something we have to die to understand. Instead, heaven can be a daily reality. And it's this experience of heaven in the here and now, this ongoing encounter of the loving embrace of our Father God that I want to discuss in this book.

It's not an easy thing to explain. Perhaps the best way I can describe it is by talking about the relationship I have with my three children.

Every Monday night is date night for my wife, Jeri, and me. We leave our three children with a baby-sitter, go out to dinner and spend some time alone with each other.

When we get back home and walk into our house, the kids often run up to us, grab us and say, "Mommy, Daddy, I love you!" They hug us. We kiss them. Even if it's just for a few minutes, we have a wonderful time of expressing our love to one another.

There have been times when I've left the room for 20 minutes or so and the whole episode repeats itself when I come back into the room. As soon as they see me they run up to me, grab me and tell me that they missed me while I was gone.

They love me. I love them. I don't mistreat them. And they don't say mean things about me behind my back. We have a pure and beautiful relationship. And that makes us happy to see each other. Spending time together is a real joy. I know this all sounds simple, perhaps even elementary, but it's the best way for me to get my point across.

This, my friend, is the kind of relationship we can all have with God. God loves us with a pure and powerful love. If we love Him back, there's no reason we shouldn't experience a taste of heaven now and spend eternity in heaven, along with the angels, who as Jesus tells us, "always see the face of my Father in heaven" (Matthew 18:10).

GETTING IT RIGHT

When I was young, I used to drive a blue 1966 Volkswagen "bug." This car was small, it was slow...but it was mine. I could put a dollar's worth of gas in the tank and that car would take me wherever I wanted to go.

Unfortunately, on one occasion I forgot to put oil in the engine. I can still remember the day I was driving down Memorial Parkway in my hometown of Huntsville, Alabama, when my little blue car began making a whole lot more noise than usual. My crankcase had dried up. The bug had slung a rod.

I called the repair shop, told them to haul my car back to my garage, and asked them to give me an estimate of what it would cost to fix it. When they said repairs would run several hundred dollars, I decided I would fix the car myself.

Immediately, a nonmechanically inclined friend and I put my beloved car up on concrete blocks, grabbed a few tools and began dismantling that Volkswagen piece by piece. At first I was very careful, placing every bolt, nut and washer and each piece of metal in a specially designated spot on the garage floor. I knew where everything had come from, and thought I would know where each piece would have to go when I put it back together.

But after unscrewing about 50 bolts, I became a lot less conscientious. First I started mixing pieces together. Soon I was piling pieces of Volkswagen up in large, messy heaps on the floor.

Before long, I grew so frustrated that I lost interest in the project. Next, I began ignoring the problem in my garage altogether. After the heaps of metal and steel and rubber had sat there for a year, I paid a hauling company to take it all away.

As the truck carried off my massive mess, I remember asking myself why I had ever begun working on the car to begin with. I had no training as a mechanic. Sure, I could tell when my car sounded funny, but I didn't know the first thing about fixing it. How did I convince myself I was a mechanic? What in the world had I been thinking?

Friend, that's the way many of us are concerning heaven. We say we want to make it to heaven; we think we're probably going to heaven, but we don't really know how to get there from here. We're a little fuzzy about some of the details. And once we really start looking at the subject carefully, we realize there's a whole lot more to it than we originally imagined.

I hope this book is going to put heaven into focus for you.

My whole purpose in this book is to show you the way to heaven. I'm not there yet myself, but I'm on the road. I can see it plainly in the distance.

If you came up to me on the street and asked me how to get to New York or Los Angeles, I would get out a map and do my best to point you in the right direction. In this book, I want to help point you toward heaven. That's where I'm headed, and I would like for you to make it there, too.

HOPE OF A HEREAFTER

In 1991, a four-year-old boy named Conor fell to his death from the 53rd floor of a Manhattan apartment building. Conor's father, musician Eric Clapton, was devastated by his son's death. In the process of grieving over his loss, Clapton wrote the moving "Tears in Heaven," a song that touched millions of listeners and expressed both a father's sadness over the death of a loved one and his hope for an eventual reunion beyond the grave.

In the song, Clapton wonders whether his son will recognize him in heaven, and whether the two will be able to hold each other's hands once again. He's more certain about one thing: Heaven is a place of peace. He sings in the closing line, "And I know, there'll be no more tears in heaven."

There are no Scripture references in the song, but the idea of heaven as a place without tears could have come straight from John's Revelation: "He will wipe every tear from their eyes. There will be no more death or mourning or crying or pain, for the old order of things has passed away" (Revelation 21:4).

One of the reasons this song was so popular is that the vast majority of people believe in some kind of heaven, and most think that they will be reunited with lost loved ones there.

TIME magazine produced an eight-page cover story about heaven in 1997. For the article, TIME joined with cable news channel CNN to conduct a poll on people's views of the afterlife. In the poll, 88 percent of people answered yes to the question, Do you believe you will meet friends and family members in heaven when you die?[1]

George Gallup Jr. has been surveying North Americans' attitudes about religion for decades. A 1994 Gallup poll found that belief in heaven remains strong, with 90 percent of people saying there is such a place.[2] In addition, in a 1996 poll, 80 percent of people understand that they will stand before God on Judgment Day and will be held accountable for their sins.[3]

The thought of Judgment Day scares some people silly, but it doesn't scare most people, according to the Gallup survey. Of those surveyed, 78 percent said they believed they had an "excellent" or "good" chance of making it to heaven.[4]

An interesting poll taken with some of the United States' richest people revealed they would pay top dollar—up to $640,000—for a place in heaven. Sorry, friend, it's not for sale...at any price.[5]

I think it's exciting that so many people believe in heaven, a place God tells us about in the Bible. And I'm glad that so many people are aware they will face God's judgment, a subject evangelists have been preaching about for centuries.

Only God knows whether 78 percent of us will be going to heaven. But in this book, I want to do everything I can to let you know all you can about heaven, and improve your chances of getting there.

HARPS AND HALOS?

Over the centuries, people have developed some interesting ideas about heaven. One of the more common concepts is that the streets of heaven are paved with gold. Other people think of life in heaven as similar to life on earth, only bigger and better. I suppose for them the phrase "mansions in heaven" suggests big palatial houses—only you don't have to clean the carpet or wash the windows.

TIME magazine's poll found that 43 percent of people believe that heaven is populated by people (or angels) playing harps, while 36 percent say its inhabitants wear shining halos.[6]

Back when I was trying to fix my VW, I should have consulted an expert mechanic or read the repair manual. Now, when I have questions about heaven, or about other subjects that God understands a whole lot better than anybody else does, I look in the Bible for answers. When we turn to the Bible with our questions about heaven and who will go there, we learn that there are 10 important things we need to know.

Heaven Is Where God Lives

We don't know where heaven is. Centuries ago, people thought it was in the clouds. Today, many still believe it's "up there" somewhere. We may never know heaven's precise location, but one thing we can be sure of is that it is God's dwelling place.

Jesus told us as much Himself, when He taught His disciples how to pray in a section of the Bible we now call "The Lord's Prayer":

"Pray, then, in this way: 'Our Father who art in heaven, hallowed be Thy name'" (Matthew 6:9, *NASB*).

Heaven Is Where God's Throne Is

God is the sovereign ruler over the entire cosmos. Instead of having an earthly capital, or working from a cramped office somewhere, He rules from heaven.

David, who knew a few things about being a king himself, tells us: "The LORD is in His holy temple; the LORD'S throne is in heaven" (Psalm 11:4, *NASB*).

The Spiritually "Clean" Will Go to Heaven

I believe God wants everyone to go to heaven. And apparently just about everybody wants to go there. Unfortunately, not everyone who wants to will go there.

What kind of person will be received by God? Again, it is David who has the information we need: "Who may ascend into the hill of the LORD? And who may stand in His holy place? He who has clean hands and a pure heart, who has not lifted up his soul to falsehood, and has not sworn deceitfully. He shall receive a blessing from the LORD and righteousness from the God of his salvation" (Psalm 24:3-5, *NASB*).

You Can "Invest" in Heaven Before You Get There

Suppose you had some money you wanted to invest in the stock market. If you're smart, you would invest your money in a company that had a bright future, not one that was going out of business the next day.

In the same way, we can send treasures to heaven even before we get there by the choices we make and the way we live our lives. As Jesus told His disciples: "Lay up for yourselves treasures in heaven,

ONLY THOSE WHO ARE HUNGRY FOR GOD AND ACKNOWLEDGE THEIR SPIRITUAL POVERTY AND NEED WILL SEE HEAVEN.

where neither moth nor rust destroys, and where thieves do not break in or steal; for where your treasure is, there will your heart be also" (Matthew 6:20,21, *NASB*).

Many Will Live in Heaven

We don't know how many people will be in heaven, but Jesus tells us that it will be many: "And I say to you, that many shall come from east and west, and recline [at the table] with Abraham, and Isaac, and Jacob, in the kingdom of heaven" (Matthew 8:11, *NASB*).

Heaven Is the Believer's Inheritance

If your father dies and leaves you his house in his will, you will receive that house, no matter what anyone says. You are his child, and he has elected that the house be given to you.

Likewise, God has reserved a place in heaven for you, and He invites us "to [obtain] an inheritance [which is] imperishable and undefiled and will not fade away, reserved in heaven for you" (1 Peter 1:4, *NASB*).

Heaven Is for the "Poor in Spirit"

Throughout history, brave soldiers have claimed that their military victories would secure them a place in God's kingdom. And powerful men of business have assumed they will be as famous after death as they were while they were alive. But God has news for us: Only those who are hungry for God and acknowledge their spiritual poverty and need will see heaven.

As Jesus told His disciples in a portion of the Gospel of Matthew called The Beatitudes, "Blessed are the poor in spirit, for theirs is the kingdom of heaven" (Matthew 5:3, *NASB*).

Our Names Can Be Written in Heaven

We may not know what our eternal destiny holds in store for us, but God knows. As Jesus tells us: "Rejoice that your names are recorded in heaven" (Luke 10:20, *NASB*).

God Wants to Give Us Heaven

Eternal life is not something God is hoarding. God is not a miser who only shares what He has with a few. Instead, He desires to share His riches with all of us.

At the end of one of the most beautiful passages of Scripture, after Jesus has told His disciples not to worry about tomorrow, or what clothes they will wear, He tells them not to worry about heaven either: "Do not be afraid, little flock, for your Father has chosen gladly to give you the kingdom" (Luke 12:32, *NASB*).

In Heaven We Will Enjoy the Presence of God

And finally, experiencing the joys of heaven is not about walking down streets of gold or living in big mansions. Instead, when I think of heaven, I think of seeing Jesus face-to-face and spending the rest of my existence in the presence of God.

As Paul tells us, "Now we see but a poor reflection as in a mirror; then we shall see face to face. Now I know in part; then I shall know fully, even as I am fully known" (1 Corinthians 13:12).

Deep down we all desire this kind of intimacy with God, and I want you to know that it's something we can experience now.

HEAVEN OR HELL?

Perhaps it should come as no great surprise, but *TIME* magazine's poll found that far fewer people believe in hell than believe in heaven. But just as believing in something doesn't make it so, *disbelieving* in something doesn't make it disappear. And just because folks don't like the idea of hell does not mean it doesn't exist.

The vast majority of people feel certain they will be going to heaven, but what makes them so sure? There's a verse in the Bible that paints a much different picture. "Small is the gate and narrow the road that leads to life," Jesus told His followers, "and only a few find it" (Matthew 7:14).

God wants everyone to be in heaven, and He even sent His Son Jesus to help us get there. But everyone isn't going to make it to heaven, friend. Unfortunately, that's just not what's going to happen. And the reason is really very simple. It is sin that causes heaven to be closed for some. I wish it were more complex, because then maybe people would get it, but it's really amazingly simple. The problem isn't with God; it's with us. As the prophet Isaiah tells us:

> Surely the arm of the Lord is not too short to save,
> nor his ear too dull to hear.

But your iniquities have separated you from your God;

your sins have hidden his face from you,

so that he will not hear (Isaiah 59:1,2).

It's our sin, our disobedience, and our hardness of heart that close heaven's door to us.

So far, we've been talking about heaven as a place where people go after death. But there's a present dimension of heaven, too. Heaven and hell aren't just "then" and "there," they are "here" and "now." And beginning today, we can experience the joys of heaven every day, or our lives can be hell on earth.

Sadly, for millions of people, heaven is closed already. The result is inner torment, sleepless nights, anxiety, worry, paranoia, shame, strife and war. This is the reason I write, and it's why I have such a burden for you, even though I may not have ever met you.

The other night, during revival services, a young man came to me after the sermon. His eyes were hollow and glassy. There was sadness and resignation etched on his face. Then he pulled up his sleeve to reveal the dark marks up and down his left arm. With a tone of pleading in his voice, he asked, "Can your God help me with my addiction?"

I pulled up my own sleeve, took his hand, and placed it on my arm. "Put your finger right there," I told him. There's a lump on my arm from the days when I used to shoot morphine. One time I missed my vein, and the morphine went into my arm and hardened there like a rock. That lump will never go away. It's a physical reminder of a period of my life when I was going nowhere fast.

Even though I was standing there in church with a suit on, and this young man was in tattered old blue jeans and had dirty, matted hair, when he put his fingers on the knot on my arm, there was an immediate connection between us. He grabbed me and hugged me and squeezed me. And with tears in his eyes, he said, "You've been there! You know what I'm going through!"

I have been there, friend. I've seen more than my share of hell. And I've also experienced the reality of heaven in the here and now.

When I look into the eyes of someone like that young man and I see pain, either from drug addiction, a broken marriage, or an abused life, something inside me begins to cry because I know things don't have to be like that. The pain doesn't have to be there. Our original purpose for living was not to suffer day in and day out.

I'VE NEVER SEEN A HEARSE PULLING A U-HAUL TRAILER. THE ONLY THING I CAN TAKE TO HEAVEN WITH ME IS OTHER PEOPLE, AND I'D LIKE YOU TO COME ALONG.

God had a much better plan when He created us. He gave us innocence; purity of thought; an amazement with the beauty of creation; feelings of love and closeness for our family, our friends and the world. But for many of us, that precious innocence has been abused or stolen. We live in darkness and fear instead of the brilliance of God's grace.

That's why I hurt inside for people.

I care about your life here on earth, and I care about what's going to happen to you after you die. I want to do something about it. I can't take any of my possessions to heaven with me when I die. I've never seen a hearse pulling a U-Haul trailer. The only thing I can take to heaven with me is other people, and I'd like you to come along.

IT'S UP TO YOU

God desires more than anything else to open the door of heaven to us. He wants us to experience life here on earth in abundance. He want us to have peace on earth, joy in our hearts and hope for the future.

Like a good father, He wants to take care of His children. He has done His part, and now we must do ours. He is faithful; we are the ones who have been unfaithful. He will never leave or forsake us; we often leave or forsake Him.

I'm not perfect, and I'm certainly not claiming to have all the answers. I'm merely a sinner saved by God's grace, and I'm still on a journey to my heavenly home. But I've learned a lot, and I can say three things without a shadow of a doubt:

- I'm going to go to heaven.
- I want you to go with me.
- I can help show you the way.

As you read this book, some of the things I'm going to say will be startling to you. Some of it may seem harsh. Perhaps you could regard my words as if they were a wake-up call, a sounding alarm in the middle of a good night's sleep. Or perhaps you might see them as bright lights on a dark night.

You might feel exposed or angry, and you may want to slam the book shut or throw it across the room. I encourage you to hang in there with me and continue reading, even if it hurts. Because in the long run, I believe it will help you.

Also, I want you to know that my prayers are with you. You'll never be able to say that no one cares for your soul. I care for you, and I'm praying that God will work mightily in your life.

A MESSAGE FROM THE LORD

As I was praying about this book, the Lord gave me this word for you:

> I created you, My child, for a purpose. The time has come for its fulfillment. My purpose for your life is all that matters.
>
> Yes, I am the One to whom you will give an account. I have demands of you. I will require them of you. There are no options. I want more.
>
> Listen, My child, receive instruction and you will live.

For too long, too many of us have been doing what Bob Dylan first sang about 25 years ago: "Knock, knock, knockin' on heaven's door." The reality is that God has swung open the door of heaven. Now the rest is up to us.

Notes

1. David Van Biema, "Does Heaven Exist?" *TIME* (March 24, 1997), p. 75.
2. Telephone Gallup poll, sponsored by CNN and *U.S.A. Today*, conducted December 16 to December 18, 1994.
3. George Gallup Jr., "Religion in America...1996" (Princeton, NJ: The Princeton Religion Research Center, 1996), p. 19.
4. Ibid.
5. *USA TODAY* Snapshot, March 26, 1999, the Internet.
6. David Van Biema, "Does Heaven Exist?" *TIME* (March 24, 1997), p. 73.

Part

LIVING AND DYING UNDER A HEAVEN OF BRASS

*God loves us and wants to throw
open the door of heaven to us.
But many of us live in a state of
spiritual isolation from God.
As we'll see, the problem isn't with God,
but with us.*

2

TESTING THE WATERS

*Reality is based on unchanging
rules and universal laws.
Still, many of us spend our lives
seeing how far we can go.
But sometimes we can go too far.*

It was Thanksgiving morning, 1962. I was eight years old. As I crawled from under the blankets and looked out my bedroom window, I could see the sun glistening on the majestic pine trees surrounding our Alabama home. Everything seemed to be bathed in a warm, golden glow. The scene was part Currier and Ives, part Norman Rockwell, part Thomas Kinkade.

The next thing I knew, my nose was summoned to attention by the heavenly aroma of a large Butterball turkey in the oven. It was only nine in the morning, but Mama had already been hard at work for hours.

Wiping the sleep from my eyes, I headed up the stairs and straight for the kitchen, which was spread out before me like a glutton's paradise. A freshly baked carrot cake sat cooling on the counter. A big bag of Idaho potatoes leaned up against the kitchen sink, and I could see how in a few hours' time those spuds would be transformed into a mountain of mashed potatoes, which would then be soaked, on my plate, in light brown, fat-laden, artery-clogging gravy.

Nearby, a big bowl of Planters mixed nuts—one of my mom's regular holiday treats—seemed to be calling out, "Steve, eat me!" We're talking top-of-the-line nuts here, folks. This was not the 75 percent-peanuts bargain blends, but a varied mix of cashews, brazil nuts, pecans and all those little mystery nuts that hold the whole mixture together. It was too late for breakfast and not quite time for the big Thanksgiving feast, so I reached over and grabbed a huge handful. I enjoyed their smell, their taste, and the greasy feeling they made in my hands. I also enjoyed the warm feeling of participating in a cherished family ritual.

Sounds normal so far, but the next item I feasted on might strike you as odd. While my Mama's back was turned, I snatched a stick of butter out of the refrigerator, peeled back the waxed paper wrapper and bit into the stick like it was a big, yellow candy bar. Today, such an act would send nutritionists into a frenzy. But back then, I loved butter. (By the way, this hunger seems to be a part of the family genetic code, for my youngest daughter now has the same butter cravings. She likes to sneak a stick and lick on it like an ice cream bar.)

Mama spied me with her all-seeing eyes. She bellowed, "Stevie, put that down! It will ruin your appetite!" and shooed me out of the kitchen.

Now wide awake, and with my body's digestive system in overdrive, I vacated the kitchen and sought to entertain myself with anything that would help me to temporarily forget my powerful hunger pangs. It wasn't long before an idea popped into my head that would earn this Thanksgiving Day a unique place in the Hill family history. Soon, this holiday would witness the kind of warm, golden glow that Norman Rockwell never, ever painted.

ANGELS WITH DIRTY FACES

My older brother, George, was struggling with the same kind of hunger pangs I was. But Mama was standing guard over the grub like a prison warden, so we decided to go outside in our search for fun and excitement.

While heading to the front door, my eyes landed on a small ivory box sitting on the living room coffee table. My dad had purchased the box in Greece while serving as a captain there in the U.S. Army. In fact, our whole house was full of memorabilia and knickknacks Dad had picked up in his travels around the world. (I was even born in faraway Ankara, Turkey!) I probably could have charged my friends an admission fee to visit our house, for every wall, shelf and cabinet was adorned with trinkets from around the world.

The ivory box was more than a trinket. When my dad wanted to light one of his Camel cigarettes (unfiltered, of course), and his shiny Zippo lighter wouldn't work, he reached for that ivory box and grabbed a book of matches. Soon the air would be filled with the sulfuric smell of just-lit matches and the smoke from Dad's rich tobacco blend.

As George and I headed out the door on this beautiful Thanksgiving morning, I popped off the lid of Dad's box, grabbed a pack of matches and headed down the road to a wheat field.

George and I walked into the middle of the large field of waist-high grain, rippling in the wind like gentle waves stirred by an ocean breeze. We cleared a small spot in the field, grabbed a few fistfuls of grain and made a small pile of wheat in the middle of our clearing. Then I knelt down, struck a match and ignited what I had hoped would be a simple little campfire.

My plans went haywire when a gust of wind picked up the small flame and blew it into the surrounding field. Our feeble attempts to stomp out the blazing fire were replaced by an overwhelming dread. It looked like our entire area of Alabama might be engulfed within a few minutes.

Like any two responsible, disciplined, God-fearing kids, George and I did what anyone would have done: We ran for our lives! We charged through the basement door, up the stairs, into our bedroom, and hurriedly took out some toys so we could act as if absolutely nothing had happened. Within minutes, we could hear the sirens and high-powered engines of fire trucks approaching our field. George and I listened fearfully as the trucks came nearer and nearer.

The firemen managed to snuff out the three-acre blaze. But then, a few of the men went from house to house, seeking clues about the fire. When the doorbell rang, our hearts nearly jumped out of our chests. We strained to listen but couldn't hear what the firefighter was saying. Then Mom answered him.

NEARLY ALL OF US SEEM TO BE BORN WITH AN INNATE DESIRE TO TEST THE LIMITS OF LIFE. AND IF THOSE ARE THE BOUNDARIES, WHAT WILL HAPPEN IF WE CROSS THEM?

"I'm sorry. We don't know anything about the fire. My children have been here at the house all day."

Then Mom walked over to our room and hollered through the door to us.

"Steve? George? Do you know anything about the fire down the street?"

"What fire?" we asked in angelic-sounding voices.

Our hearts were racing. Our eyes were burning from the smoke. Our faces were covered with the grimy black residue from the fire's hot ashes. And we couldn't even smell Mama's turkey anymore. Instead, our clothes, hair and skin were permeated with the smell of burning wheat.

LIKE MOTHS TO A FLAME

Like just about every other relatively normal child, my parents had warned me hundreds of times not to play with matches. In my little eight-year-old mind, the commandment, *Thou shalt not play with matches* was right up there with others, such as, *Thou shalt not leave thine toys scattered all over the bedroom floor*, or *Thou shalt not make thine little sister cry*.

I knew the rules, and my actions that day represented direct defiance. And I suspect there is not a human being reading these words who was not involved in some similar kind of childhood prank. In fact, nearly all of us seem to be born with an innate desire to test the limits of life. From the day we're born, many of us are busy asking: Just how far can I go? And if those are the boundaries, what will happen if I cross them?

In my home—as in about 75 percent of American homes—children were raised according to some system of biblical standards. That doesn't mean all parents always applied these standards consistently or followed them in their own lives. But the vast majority of us grew up in households where firm lines were drawn and, when needed, swift punishment was handed out when the boundaries were crossed.

For me, the flaming wheat field was merely one of hundreds of incidents where I tested the waters. I knew the rules. I knew right from wrong. I chose to do what was wrong. Something inside of me wanted to find out how serious the consequences of disobedience really were.

SOME URGENT QUESTIONS FOR YOU

At this point, I would like to turn the tables and beg you to please allow me to be very direct in asking you some questions. For the next few pages, the focus won't be on me and the crazy things I did as a child (or even as a so-called "grown-up"). Instead, the emphasis will be on you, your experiences and the things that have helped make you who you are today.

In the pages that follow, I want to ask you four simple but important questions:

- Where are you from?
- Where have you been?
- Where are you now?
- Where are you going?

Please take a moment to consider these questions and weigh their implications for your life.

Where Are You From?
First I would like to ask about how you were raised. What is your family background? What is your unique heritage? Where did you originate? And do you remember any authority figures setting up rules and regulations for you to follow when you were a child?

Do you come from a Christian home? Did your mom and dad take you to church or Sunday School? My mom recently gave me a few of my Lutheran Sunday School papers she had saved from when I was younger than five years old. They were called *Little Visits with Jesus*. There were stories about Jesus, and little pictures to color. Here I was barely out of diapers and someone was already telling me that Jesus loved me and had a plan for my life. What about you?

Do you remember reading about how God gave Moses the Ten Commandments, or do you remember hearing songs about Jesus? Did you grow up learning about the beatings Jesus took across His back and the crown of thorns He wore? Did your friends and family talk to you about God? Did you pray over meals? Did mom or dad pray a blessing over your little life late at night?

That wasn't the case for Roger, who was the head of a notorious biker gang in New Orleans. I first met him after his latest run-in with the police had led to his being paroled to a Christian drug rehabilitation center in Alabama where I was working as a counselor. Roger was well over six feet tall, weighed 350 pounds and was covered with tattoos, including curse words and decorations on his eyelids. He was a *mean man.*

I still remember how he walked up to me, looked me in the eye and grumbled, "I just want you to know I hate you, and if you turn your back, I'll kill you." I wanted to kick him out, but we couldn't. The police had placed him with us, and we had to keep him.

Soon, though, something amazing happened to Roger. One month after he had threatened me, this huge man began to cry during one of our chapel services. When I asked who wanted to receive Jesus as Savior and Lord, Roger gave his life to Jesus, just as hundreds had done before him. Looking at me through his tears, Roger said, "Brother Steve, I want to testify." And as his sad story spilled out, I gained a new perspective on this hulk of a man:

I just want you all to know that I'm really not that bad. Inside I've got a soft heart. When I was four years old, my mama kicked me out of the house. I had to learn to survive on the streets of New Orleans. I've lived on the streets all my life. I learned at an early age how to hustle for a living. When Mardi Gras came around, I learned how to pick pockets and con the tourists. No one ever taught me right from wrong.

Everybody has a story. Roger's was about a life void of love and a little boy roaming the streets without any rules. What is your story?

Maybe you never heard of God or church until a man knocked on the door and asked your parents if a church bus could come by and pick you up on Sundays. You heard your dad say, "Fine with me, if it gets the little monster out of my hair for a while." The next Sunday morning, you and dozens of other kids were on your way to a place the bus driver called "the house of God."

Perhaps you were raised in some other form of religion. Maybe your parents made their living reading tarot cards or telling fortunes to a steady stream of strangers who paraded through your home. Others may have been raised by a mom who was always dabbling in this, checking out that, running to astrology, seeking answers in a horoscope, or doing nearly anything to find out what the next day of her dreary life was going to be like.

Maybe you were born into a Jewish family, and you can still vividly remember attending synagogue every Sabbath, eating kosher food, celebrating the Holy Days, and then performing your bar mitzvah when you turned thirteen.

What's your story?

Maybe you're not from the United States. Perhaps you were born in Japan and raised a Buddhist. As a young child you visited the temple to offer fruit, flowers and incense to Buddha, and in your home was a small altar where you and your family would chant prayers each day.

Perhaps you were born in rural Taiwan and reared in Taoism. Your parents read to you from the teachings of Confucius and Lao-tzu and taught you how to meditate and how to honor your parents and your dead ancestors.

Maybe you grew up in Lebanon or Egypt and were brought up in Islam. Five times a day you bowed down in prayer, facing Mecca, the holy city where your father once went on a pilgrimage. You fasted during the daylight hours for the month of Ramadan.

Perhaps you're from Germany or Finland. If so, chances are you were brought up as a Lutheran, complete with baptism as a newborn child, services of the Lord's Supper, lessons from Luther's catechism and confirmation at age twelve. (I remember being caught cheating on the final exam, but the pastor overlooked it and confirmed me anyway.)

Maybe you grew up in America, learning about God and moral living in the Church of Jesus Christ of Latter Day Saints. When your brother was 19, he left for South America for two years' service as a missionary. No one you knew from the church drank alcohol or coffee, and no one smoked tobacco either.

Maybe you attended weekly meetings at the Kingdom Hall of Jehovah's Witnesses. Your parents went door-to-door, giving away *Watchtower* magazines. You were embarrassed when you couldn't celebrate Christmas with the other kids, or when they stood in class each morning to recite the Pledge of Allegiance, and your religion prohibited you from joining in.

What's your story?

Maybe you grew up in a religious vacuum. Perhaps your mom and dad were drug addicts in the sixties. In the seventies they cleaned up their acts a bit. In the eighties they made some money. And now they are caught up in a social scene where drunkenness, drug use and sexual immorality are considered chic. They are totally caught up in the pleasures of this life and have no interest in God.

Where are you from? Your past may not be perfect, and there are few people alive who wouldn't change something about their upbringing if they had the chance. But it always helps to know where we're coming from.

Where Have You Been?

Where you have been has less to do with your parents and your upbringing, and more to do with what you have been doing with your life. There are two stories from the Bible that may help you answer this second question.

The Gospel of Luke describes a young man who typifies millions of Americans today. Those who know the story call him the prodigal son. He was reared with everything a boy could want. He had a good home, good food, plenty of everything and a father who loved him dearly. But upbringing wasn't enough. Not content with his arrangement, the son asked for his inheritance early, then took the money and ran. Soon he had squandered everything on wild living.

The Bible's first story about people for whom everything wasn't enough is found in the book of Genesis. Adam and Eve had it made. The world was under their control. They were at peace with each other and with their Creator. Living in the Garden of Eden, they enjoyed every imaginable kind of fruit and flowers. You could say they had it "made in the shade."

God only gave Adam and Eve one rule, and it was a simple one: They were not to eat the fruit of a certain tree. But thinking they needed more than the wealth they already had, they broke that one

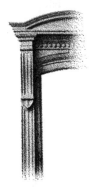

EVERY SUNDAY MORNING, CHURCHES FROM COAST TO COAST ARE FULL. BUT SITTING IN CHURCH WON'T MAKE YOU A CHRISTIAN ANY MORE THAN SITTING IN A GARAGE WILL MAKE YOU A CAR.

rule, believing the lie that the consequences wouldn't be so bad. They miscalculated. Instead of dining with deity, instead of fellowshipping with their Father, they were off in some no-man's-land, dealing with the devil.

So now we know where the prodigal son had been. We know where Adam and Eve had been. Now I'm asking you, where have you been?

Have you, like millions of others, broken past God's moral and ethical boundaries only to find yourself wandering through life with no accountability? Have you tested the waters, taking a swan dive into the deep, dark sea of sensuality?

Have you been glued to a La-Z-Boy, with an ergonomically shaped remote molded to your hand to control a 25-inch box spewing out vile abominations in living color?

Have you been in the backseat of a car, steaming up the windows with someone who doesn't really care about you? Or have you been in the back room with a porno magazine, arousing your passions? How about that date with a same-sex friend who claims you were born with those tendencies? Or have you been breaking God's laws by lying to your boss or stealing from your employer?

If you're running from God, playing religion won't help you. Every Sunday morning, churches from coast to coast are full. But sitting in a church won't make you a Christian any more than sitting in a garage will make you a car. Ask yourself this: Is your church attendance making any change in your life? God doesn't want you to sanctimoniously sing "Amazing Grace," then walk out of church and curse your spouse, abuse your kids, rip apart the preacher and fight for a good parking spot at a nearby restaurant.

That's religion, friend, and it stinks to high heaven. God is not in it. In fact, I believe the devil is busy trying to pacify the average lukewarm churchgoer. Satan likes people who sing a few hymns, drop a few coins in the offering basket and head out the door without their lives ever being changed by God.

Pastors tell me that when their churches sponsor fishing trips, half the men in the church show up at 5:00 A.M. But when there's a morning prayer meeting, everyone says, "Pastor, I just can't get up that early."

That's religion, not Christianity. What's the difference? Someone once put it like this: Religion is hanging around the Cross; but Christianity is getting on the Cross.

Where have you been, my friend? What's in your past? Where have your eyes been? Where has your mouth been? Where have your legs taken you? Which way are you headed?

Where Are You Now?

Last time we checked on the prodigal son, he was living high on the hog. But the good times didn't last, and soon he was living *with* the hogs! The last place a nice Jewish boy should be is in a pigpen, slopping pigs, but that's exactly where the prodigal ended up. It proves one thing: The devil will promise you everything and leave you with nothing.

The prodigal chose to leave his own family. Maybe that's where you are right now. Perhaps you've left the heritage of your grandma and your grandpa, your mom and your dad, and now you're spinning wildly out of control. You've wandered away from the true and simple rules of life and are now entangled in a merciless web of sin, paranoia and depression. You'd do anything if the God of your childhood would come help you once again.

Where are you now, my friend? What kind of pigpen are you living in? What are you chewing on? What is the devil giving you? Like the prodigal, all of us must get to a place where we realize our condition and have a deep desire to do something about it.

Perhaps you can remember back to a time when you were in church. Things weren't perfect, but they were good. You went after God. You sang in the choir. But somebody did something that upset you, and you left church, taking your family with you. Now your life is in shambles. You don't love God anymore. You don't love anyone or anything anymore, including yourself. Welcome to the devil's pigsty.

Do you know Jesus or not? Are you near Him or far from Him? Remember Adam and Eve? What a story! One minute they were walking in the garden with God, and the next minute they were hiding from their Maker. Are you walking with God or hiding from Him? Are you less troubled than you once were about right and wrong?

It may be uncomfortable, but I'm asking you, Where are you right now? Please be truthful, because if you don't know where you are, you won't be able to answer the next question either.

Where Are You Going?

Before our self-examination concludes, please allow me to ask you one more question: Where are you going? The previous questions have focused on where you are now or where you've been in the past. Now it's time to look to the future.

I'll tell you how the prodigal answered that question. After coming to his senses, he said, "I'm going home. I'm sick of living with the pigs, and I'm going back home to my father." How about you? Are you tired of the life you're living? Are you ready to return to your heavenly Father?

Things didn't turn out so well for Adam and Eve. They were kicked out of the Garden of Eden, and God placed angels at the garden's gates to enforce the ban.

I've often wondered what would have happened if Adam and Eve had repented. What if, after eating the forbidden fruit, they had fallen on their faces and cried out to God, "Look what we've done! We've broken the only rule You told us to obey. We've sinned against You, our Maker. Forgive us, God."

Being outside of paradise isn't any fun. Finding oneself outside of the will of God is a horrible place to be. But like Adam and Eve, many of us have tested the waters, broken the rules and found ourselves alienated from God. This part of the book is entitled, "Living and Dying Under a Heaven of Brass." These words come straight from the Bible:

> But it shall come to pass, if thou wilt not hearken unto the voice of the LORD thy God,...And thy heaven that is over thy head shall be brass, and the earth that is under thee shall be iron (Deuteronomy 28:15,23, *KJV*).

That's where many of us are, but is that where you want to be? Where are you going?

THE CALL OF THE CONSCIENCE

God sees all that we do—the good,
the bad and the ugly.
And He has given us all a built-in
navigational system which can help us
distinguish right from wrong, light from dark.

Before God reached down and saved me, I spent a fair amount of time running from the law.

I'll never forget one Friday night. I went to a bar, got stinking drunk and ended up in a fight. I don't remember many of the details, but I do remember regaining consciousness the next morning in a jail cell. My head was pounding, and I thought to myself, *This is one doozy of a hangover!* But then I felt my face. There was a big bump on my forehead and dried blood caked all around it.

My mom came and bailed me out, as she often did. (My father had died of a heart attack when I was 16.) A few days later, police investigators pulled me over as I was driving down the road and ordered me to report to the courthouse. Upon my arrival, they took me into an interrogation room full of detectives, one of whom looked me straight in the face and said, "Tell me everything you know about the murder."

A wealthy woman from Huntsville, Alabama, had been murdered Friday night, and apparently I matched the description of the killer. "How did you plan it?" the detective asked me.

"But I didn't," I said. For once in my life I knew I hadn't actually done the bad things somebody was accusing me of, and I proclaimed my innocence with everything in me.

I had a clear conscience, and I must have made my point, for after a half hour of questioning, a detective looked at me and then looked at the officers in the room and declared, "This man didn't do it. You can let him go."

I wasn't so lucky the next time. I was arrested in a drug bust and charged with selling narcotics—a felony. I was guilty as sin, but I was sure my innocent-looking face would impress the judge, or that my high-powered lawyer could get me off on a technicality. But then the prosecuting attorney reached into his briefcase, pulled out a half-inch stack of legal-sized papers and began reading to the judge. It went something like this:

> At 6:00 P.M. on the evening in question, defendant Stephen Hill left his house in a blue Volkswagen, which was missing two hubcaps, and drove to the nearby Winn-Dixie supermarket parking lot. The defendant parked near a dark green dumpster, where he waited until approximately 6:30 P.M. At that time, a black Ford van with two white males pulled alongside the defendant's car. After a few moments of conversation, the defendant handed a large plastic package to the driver of the other car, who then handed a stack of currency to the defendant. At approximately 6:40 P.M., the defendant returned to his home....

And that was just page one! I sat in amazement as the prosecutor recited nearly every major detail from that one week of my life. I hadn't realized it before, but someone had been watching my every move.

That's the way it is for all of us, only it isn't police investigators keeping an eye on us; it is God, who sees all things from heaven. What does God see when He looks at you and me? And how can we make sure He likes what He sees in us? These are some of the questions we'll explore in this chapter.

THE TWO SIDES OF THE MATTER

Each one of us has two distinct sides. There's the side we want others to see, and then there's the side we would all prefer to keep hidden.

Part of this is as natural as wanting to put our best foot forward. For example, people who aren't good at academics like to show you their athletic trophies; and folks who can't dribble a basketball without hitting their own toes like to show you all the good grades on their report cards.

Most working people don't get up in the morning, jump out of bed, hop into the car and drive straight to work. I don't know about you, but my fresh-out-of-bed side is not the side I want to reveal to everyone I work with. My hair is usually matted down and poofed off to one side. My face is lined with pillow imprints. My eyes are full of sleep dust. And my breath smells like a small rodent crawled into my mouth and died there. (Have you ever experienced this?)

I love my staff. I want them to keep working with me. So I don't scare them off by going to the office immediately after getting out of bed. Instead, I make a detour through the bathroom, where I spend some time making myself presentable.

There's nothing wrong with getting cleaned up and dressed up for work. But there's a deeper problem concerning the way some of us deal with the two sides of our lives. Most of us have a carefully crafted public side that we like to parade to the world around us. And then there is a dark, private side that we try to hide from others, even from God.

There are two fascinating accounts from the Old and New Testaments of the Bible that help us gain a godly understanding of our public and private sides.

Kings and Adulterers

History books record the fact that King David was Israel's foremost ruler. And as with all politicians, David probably loved the pomp that came along with his position. How could he resist the allure of being out in public and having thousands of people cry out, "Hail, King David! Blessings on God's anointed!"

But there was a much darker side of his life, which David attempted to hide. This story begins in 2 Samuel, chapter 11. In my Bible, this chapter has the headline, "David's Great Sin."

David lived in a large and opulent palace. One night when he was out walking on the roof of the palace, he saw a neighbor—a woman named Bathsheba—who was taking a bath. Bathsheba was a beautiful woman, and her husband, a godly man named Uriah, was off fighting in one of David's wars. David summoned her and slept with her. But it didn't end there, because Bathsheba became pregnant. Isn't it amazing how unplanned consequences conspire to complicate our lives?

In an effort to keep his sin hidden, David devised a hideous plan. He commanded that Uriah be put in the front lines of battle, where he was killed by the enemy. David thought Uriah's death would conceal his sin from everyone, but there's one thing each of us needs to remember: There are always at least three witnesses to everything we do: the Father, the Son and the Holy Spirit.

God had seen David's sin, and He sent a righteous prophet named Nathan to confront David. Nathan began by telling David a seemingly innocent story about a rich man and a poor man. The rich man had many flocks and herds, but the poor man had nothing but one small ewe lamb, which his family loved and cared for. When a traveler came to visit, the rich man didn't butcher one of the many sheep he owned; he stole the poor man's ewe and served it to his guest.

The story made David angry, and he said to Nathan, "The man who did this deserves to die!"

But Nathan responded with the message God had sent him to deliver: "You are the man! You struck down Uriah the Hittite with the sword and took his wife to be your own!"

David suddenly saw that God had exposed his secret side, and he cried out, "I have sinned against the Lord!"

It's not just kings who try to cover their tracks. In the Gospel of John, Jesus shows us how religious folks often like to publicly parade their religiosity but keep their secret sins hidden from public view. Jesus was never too fond of people who liked to show off to other folks how religious they were. He said, "Whoever exalts himself will be humbled, and whoever humbles himself will be

> INSTEAD OF TRYING TO PRETEND WE'RE PERFECT, WE SHOULD LET JESUS SEE ALL OF WHO WE ARE—THE GOOD, THE BAD AND THE JUST PLAIN UGLY. AFTER ALL, HE ALREADY KNOWS EVERYTHING ABOUT US.

exalted" (Matthew 23:12). One day Jesus was teaching near the Temple when some self-righteous Jews brought to Him a woman who was an adulteress and challenged Jesus to condemn her.

Instead of responding immediately, Jesus bent down and wrote something on the ground with His finger. The Bible doesn't tell us what He wrote, but my wife, Jeri, thinks it might be the words, "Where is the man?" For adultery is never a one-party act.

Then Jesus straightened up and announced: "If any one of you is without sin, let him be the first to throw a stone at her" (John 8:7). The judgmental zeal of the group evaporated, and soon each member silently walked away, until Jesus was left alone with the woman.

"Woman, where are they?" He asked. "Has no one condemned you?"

"No one, Sir," she said.

"Then neither do I condemn you," Jesus declared. "Go now and leave your life of sin."

In this amazing encounter, the person whose sin was publicly exposed was forgiven by God. But the self-righteous accusers, those who tried to present a carefully crafted image of sinless perfection, were left with no relief for their inner guilt and shame.

All of us have a dark side. Instead of trying to pretend we are perfect by hiding it from our friends and from God, we should let Jesus see all of who we are—the good, the bad and the just plain ugly. After all, He already knows everything about us. Jesus didn't die only for your good side, He died for your dark side, too.

Smelly Junk in Dark Corners

I remember the house I grew up in had a two-car garage that was divided into two halves. One side, the bright side, was where we kept the good family car. This side was where the garage door was usually left open, letting plenty of light into the space.

The other side was dark and dingy. This was where my dad parked some old clunker of a car he had bought for $200, as well as lots of other junk we had collected. Sunlight rarely penetrated the gloom. There were a few small electric lights, but they were never bright enough to illuminate the darkness. Only about once a year was this side of the garage cleaned or swept out. The floor was heavily spotted with oil leaks from old cars. Everything seemed to be buried under layers of dust. The corners were full of spider webs, and the air was permeated by a damp, musty smell. That side of the garage was dirty and creepy, and I did everything I could to stay out of it.

I think of that garage sometimes when I find myself reading a verse in the Bible that has always made so much sense to me. It's just three verses past John 3:16, which is probably one of the most famous verses in the Bible ("For God so loved the world that he gave his one and only Son"), but the verse I'm thinking of is not quite so rosy in its outlook. Jesus said: "Light has come into the world, but men loved darkness instead of light because their deeds were evil" (John 3:19).

When I think of the "dark side" of that garage, I am reminded of how the darkness concealed all the spider webs, dust and grime. Remember King David? He tried everything he could think of to keep his private sins from coming to light. And isn't that what many of us do on a regular basis?

THE BATTLE FOR THE SOUL

Theologians can argue for years about what the really important themes in the Bible are, but I think one of the recurring truths is the cosmic battle between light and darkness. From the very beginning of the Bible, when God says, "Let there be light" and His word illumines a dark and chaotic cosmos, to the very end of the Bible, where the forces of goodness triumph over the forces of evil, God's book is one long story of the ongoing battle between light and darkness.

If we narrow the focus a bit, we can see there is also a battle between light and darkness going on in our own souls. Every day, each of us is bombarded by temptations. That's when the inner battle begins, as we wrestle with whether or not to succumb.

I remember being on a plane trip with my good friend Mike Brown. We had spoken together at a rally up in Montgomery, Alabama, and were flying back home to Pensacola. We were talking about ministry around the world when a certain brother's name came up. Before I knew what had happened, I had cut this brother down by saying critical things about his ministry. It took me just a few choice words to lay this man low. But almost as soon as the words were out of my mouth, a sense of deep guilt and conviction came over me. That was the work of God, convicting me through my conscience that what I had done was wrong. I felt horrible, and I turned to Mike and said, "Please forgive me, Mike." That day, my dark, cutting words were illuminated and annihilated by the light of Christ.

I have seen people struggle with the temptation to strike back in anger or rage when their faith in Jesus is questioned or attacked. The Brownsville revival has come in for its share of criticism from those who claim God is not at work here. Instead of becoming defensive or nasty, those who are criticized need to respond in love. Instead of calling critics "idiots" or "God-haters," they should say, "Hey, brother, let me tell you what God did for me and my family through the revival."

One of the most prevalent enticements many people face today is sexual temptation. We live in a thoroughly sex-saturated society where movies, TV shows, music videos, magazines, Internet sites and advertising all traffic in sexual images. This nation is like a bunch of animals in heat!

Everyone has probably seen at least one commercial for an automobile featuring a scantily clad woman sitting on the hood or standing by its side. Cars are expensive purchases, my friend, and it seems you would want to think carefully before spending thousands of dollars on a new model. But advertising tries to bypass our rational nature and appeal to our animal instincts. Instead of thinking, *I wonder how this car's gas mileage is?*, some people are seduced by the provocatively dressed woman and start fantasizing, *I wonder if women like that would love me if I had a snazzy car?* Women in skimpy clothing are mild compared to some of the pornographic photos and blatantly sexual "chat" anyone can encounter on the Internet. In recent years, some "virtual" perverts have even used their computers to store and transmit child pornography, believing they were immune to prosecution. I was so thankful to read in the papers that in September 1998, police in America and 11 other countries raided the homes of more than 100 on-line pornographers who exchanged sexual photos of children, some as young as two years old. This was the largest child pornography raid of its kind. Sin never changes, my friend, even though new technologies give sinners new methods. It's just another variation on the theme of darkness versus light.

So many of the people who have visited the Brownsville revival have been struggling with sexual sins like masturbation, fornication and adultery. They think nobody knows about their secret sins, but you don't have to be a celebrity, a president or a congressman to realize the truth of these words from Moses: "You may be sure that your sin will find you out" (Numbers 32:23).

Bringing Darkness to Light

In the battle between good and evil, Satan knows all about darkness. That's where he lives and works, and that's where he tempts us to hide our dark deeds from the piercing light of God. Or as Paul puts it in 2 Corinthians 4:4,

> The god of this age has blinded the minds of unbelievers, so that they cannot see the light of the gospel of the glory of Christ, who is the image of God.

But there's one thing the devil conveniently forgets to tell people: Everything will one day come to light. Just as the devil works in deception and darkness, God is truth and light, and He works to bring all things out into the light of day. As Jesus says in Matthew 10:26, "There is nothing concealed that will not be disclosed, or hidden that will not be made known."

You might be able to cheat on school exams and get away with it for now, but you might not be as successful concealing your shame or covering over your ignorance of things you should have learned in school. You might be able to hide your adultery from your spouse for a while, but pregnancy and sexually transmitted diseases (STDs) are much harder to conceal. According to recent studies, there are millions of unplanned pregnancies and new cases of STDs in America every year. You may even succeed in temporarily keeping your boss from knowing you are sleeping on the job or stealing money from the cash drawer. But one day all will come to light. Every deed will be revealed.

Jesus proclaims, "What you have said in the dark will be heard in the daylight, and what you have whispered in the ear in the inner rooms

NO ONE ENJOYS HAVING HIS SINS EXPOSED, BUT IF WE WANT TO FOLLOW GOD, WE MUST BE WILLING TO LET HIS LIGHT SHINE INTO OUR SOULS AND ILLUMINATE DARK CORNERS.

will be proclaimed from the roofs" (Luke 12:3). Or as Paul tells us, when the Lord comes, "He will bring to light what is hidden in darkness and will expose the motives of men's hearts" (1 Corinthians 4:5).

No one enjoys having his sins exposed, but if we want to follow God, we must be willing to let His light shine into our souls and illuminate dark corners that we had previously sought to hide. King David didn't enjoy having Nathan the prophet expose his adultery with Bathsheba or his murdering of Uriah. But once his sins had been brought to light, David made the right response. After he was confronted, David prayed a prayer of penitence, recorded in Psalm 51:

> Have mercy on me, O God,
>> according to your unfailing love...
> Surely you desire truth in the inner parts;
>> you teach me wisdom in the inmost place (verses 1,6).

Elsewhere, David wrote:

> When I kept silent,
>> my bones wasted away
>> through my groaning all day long.
> For day and night
>> your hand was heavy upon me;
>> my strength was sapped
>> as in the heat of summer.
> Then I acknowledged my sin to you
>> and did not cover up my iniquity.
> I said, "I will confess
>> my transgressions to the Lord" —
>> and you forgave the guilt of my sin (Psalm 32:3-5).

Turn On the Light

Have you ever seen video footage shot with a night-vision lens? These lenses, which utilize the same technology soldiers use in their night-vision goggles, illumine dark scenes with a vivid, eerie light. Sometime I picture Jesus wearing a big pair of night-vision goggles that reveal things that we think are hidden. I picture Him that way when I read Psalm 139:12: "Even the darkness will not be dark to you; the night will shine like the day."

With His big binoculars, Jesus can see our sins, but He can also see the good things in our lives—the hours spent working at a soup kitchen, extending a hand of love to the down-and-out; the evening spent praying for our children as they sleep through the night; the difficult times of standing up for what is right while everybody else is dead set on doing what's wrong.

Jesus certainly has the ability to see our hidden sins, but wouldn't it be better if we would just allow the light of God to expose our darkness? Today, many houses have dimmer switches that can bring the light up or down gradually. When James instructs us to "resist the devil, and he will flee from you" (James 4:7), I sometimes think that resisting the devil means we need to work on turning the dimmer switch up so we can get more light while the devil is doing everything he can to take us into darkness.

We may not be faced with dramatic King David-sized sins, like murdering our lover's spouse, but even if we are, by turning the light up a notch instead of letting Satan turn it down, we can begin to live in the glory of God's light. Soon we'll be able to see things a lot more clearly. We'll have advanced warning when temptation is coming our way. We'll have less garbage hidden away in dark, dreary corners of our lives.

THE BIG BOOK AND THE BIG CAMERA

The book you are reading is approximately 200 pages long and has slightly less than 50,000 words. But the books God has been compiling since the beginning of time are so big that they boggle the mind. These books contain everything we have ever done. We read in Revelation 20:12, "The dead were judged according to what they had done as recorded in the books."

Some people believe these books are full of words and written descriptions of all the deeds in our lives. But imagine with me that they also include photos. Imagine God having the world's biggest camera and using it to take photos of us throughout out lives. He doesn't need a tripod to hold this camera steady. He doesn't need a flash attachment—His light brightens even the darkest scene. He doesn't need you to hold still and pose; His pictures are candid snapshots that capture things as they really happened. (Talk about amazing home videos! I'm sure God's video collection isn't very funny.) God takes perfect pictures day in and day out, and they show everything, my friend. Everything.

I've done my share of dark deeds in my life, and I know God saw every depressing moment. But that's not the end of the story for me, and it doesn't need to be the end of the story for you, either.

As God's photo technicians were getting ready to take the film of my life into the lab to develop it and make the prints for the big book, Jesus came up behind them and tapped them on the shoulder.

"Give me the film," He said quietly but firmly.

"But these are the photos of Steve Hill's life," they replied. "Everything that he's ever done—the good, the bad and the ugly—is captured in these photos."

"I know," Jesus replied. "But one day Steve prayed and asked Me to forgive all his sins. He invited Me into his life and asked Me to remove the darkness. My blood has cleansed him, My grace has restored him, My love has melted away his evil heart." With that, the heavenly photo technicians took the film and exposed it to the light. As a result, the film became void of images through the brilliant light of the Son of God.

The idea about the camera may be fanciful, but the message is the gospel truth. Time and time again, the Bible promises that those who turn to God will have their sins forgiven. God has put all our sins behind His back (see Isaiah 38:17). He has nailed them to the cross of Christ (see Colossians 2:14). He has blotted them out (see Isaiah 43:25). He has removed them as far as the east is from the west (see Psalm 103:12). He has cast them into the depths of the sea (see Micah 7:19).

When God created the universe, He programmed it to run on the law of right and wrong. When He created you and me, He gave us each a conscience to know the difference. Still, we messed things up. But He can forgive and forget if we want Him to. Isn't that wonderful news?

4

THE SPIRITUALITY BOOM

Today there is a growing interest in spirituality.
Much of this hunger is good, but even a starving man
shouldn't eat everything that's put before him.

During the last few years, people haven't been able to turn on the TV, listen to the radio, go to a movie or read a magazine without coming across somebody talking about spirituality.

Visit a bookstore and you can't turn around without bumping into a stack of books about prayer, meditation or death and dying. And look at some of the stories that have appeared on the covers of national magazines: "Life After Death," "The Mystery of Prayer," "Does Heaven Exist?" and "Prophecy." Even *Self,* a magazine that has previously focused on firmer tummies and thinner thighs, did a special issue on "Your Spiritual Life."

Gallup polls reveal that 96 percent of Americans believe in God.[1] And nearly two-thirds of Americans believe that religion can answer all or most of contemporary society's problems.[2]

I'm not saying that all—or even most—of this spiritual activity is Christian. It's not. And that worries some folks. They see this resurgence of spirituality as the beginning of some kind of new Dark Ages. But not me.

I think this is a tremendously exciting time to be alive. In fact, I believe we're living in one of the most important periods in human history. I even think I prefer being alive now than at the

> # EVEN THOUGH OUR CULTURE HAS ACHIEVED ALMOST UNPRECEDENTED LEVELS OF AFFLUENCE, THERE REMAINS A POWERFUL HUNGER FOR SOMETHING MORE.

time of Christ. Why? Because millions and millions of people are realizing that there is more to life than what you can experience through the five senses. They see that there's more to human existence than flesh and blood, and that there's more to life than eating, drinking and being merry. We are living in a day when people are hungry for God.

Just as I discovered 25 years ago, folks are realizing that there will never be enough drugs, alcohol and sensual pleasures to satisfy them. Even though our culture has achieved almost unprecedented levels of affluence, there remains a powerful hunger for something more. And even though ours is one of the most informed cultures the world has ever known, there remains a deep thirst for divine truth. I believe it's this hunger and thirst that make our period in history so exciting. The prophet Amos spoke of this incredible famine for truth over 2,500 years ago when, speaking for the Almighty God, he said:

"The days are coming," declares the Sovereign LORD,

"when I will send a famine through the land—

not a famine of food or a thirst for water,

but a famine of hearing the words of the LORD" (Amos 8:11).

CHECK THE LABEL FIRST

Spiritual hunger and thirst are natural and God-given, but just like physical hunger, they can lead us to consume things that aren't always good for us.

Have you ever watched any of the old Western movies? There's one scene that seems to pop up in many of those old films. The hero—let's call him Johnny DoRight—is riding across the hot desert sand on his trusty horse—let's call the horse Sundance. The sun is high in the sky, and its rays are scorching everything in sight. Even the prickly cacti that line the desert floor seem to be wilting from the lack of water and shade.

When Johnny first started riding days ago, he was chasing some bad guys or something, but right now he isn't too sure what he's doing. His head feels kind of light and fuzzy. Then Sundance, who wanted to lie down and die hours ago, finally runs out of gas and conks out on the sand. Now Johnny realizes he has to cross the rest of the burning desert on foot.

Johnny mops his sweating brow with his handy bandanna and squints through the bright rays of the sun. Suddenly, he thinks he sees an oasis in the distance. He runs, walks, then crawls the last few miles on his hands and knees until he reaches the edge of a bright blue pool of glistening water. Once he gets there, he plunges his head beneath the surface and begins drinking in the wonderful wet coolness.

As the camera pans around the oasis scene, we can see something Johnny didn't. Just five feet away from where he is quenching his thirst, there is a small primitive sign marked with a skull and crossbones. Johnny is drinking from a poisoned spring! He will be dead in a matter of moments, and his body will make a nice lunch for the dozens of vultures circling overhead. Of course, in the movies the good guy is always rescued at the last moment.

The bottom line is this: Johnny should have checked the sign before he drank, just as grocery shoppers should check the nutrition labels on food products before they buy. Sure, that cookie-dough ice cream looks yummy, but do you really want to consume a few months' worth of saturated fat in one sitting?

My greatest fear about today's spirituality boom is that people who are hungry and thirsty for God are going to crawl to any nearby waterhole that looks good, and like our dear friend Johnny,

ONE OF THE MOST IMPORTANT THINGS WE NEED TO REMEMBER AS WE GO THROUGH THE BIG HOT DESERT CALLED LIFE IS THAT NEITHER ALL PONDS NOR ALL RELIGIONS ARE CREATED EQUAL.

they're going to lap up whatever they find. But instead of meeting God, many people become entangled with some crazy cult led by a demanding dictator spouting toxic teachings. One of the most important things we need to remember as we go through the big hot desert called life is that neither all ponds nor all religions are created equal.

THE "CULT EXPLOSION"

Christianity has been around for nearly 2,000 years, but in the last few decades there has been an explosion of strange new cults in America, many of them appealing to people who are hungry for

God but believe they'll never find Him in a traditional church.

I don't often find myself agreeing with flamboyant British singing sensation Boy George, but George recently visited a church to attend the christening service of his one-year-old godson, Michael, and I can sympathize with his comments. "Churches are glorious places," he said afterwards, "but don't you wish they were a little more inviting?" George was totally confused by Anglican liturgy and theology. "Because I never go to church it was like explaining Shakespeare to a groundhog," he said.

The sexually confused George liked the priest's fashion sense but disliked "the utterly depressing hymns," saying he would "like to see live music, acoustic guitars and percussion." (Perhaps he ought to come visit the Brownsville revival some day!)

Boy George's closing comments were particularly sad, but true: "The Church badly needs a facelift because it's God's theater on Earth, and He should be packing them in."[3]

The late Dr. Walter Martin, who was a pioneering researcher of cults, coined the term "cult explosion" to describe the mushrooming interest in religious groups that are "functioning on the periphery of Christianity." Martin said there were 25 to 30 million Americans involved in cults, groups which "have their own liturgy, they have their own extra-biblical revelations, their own leaders, and they make copious use of the Bible, most always out of context."[4]

Most of the time cults operate in secrecy, but on occasion they become front-page news, as did groups led by Charles Manson in the 1970s, Jim Jones in the 1980s, and more recently, Marshall Applewhite in the 1990s.

Applewhite was the leader of a group called Heaven's Gate. In 1997, the uniformed bodies of 38 members of the group were found lying dead in their bunks in their San Diego County house. Why? Because Applewhite had convinced his followers that they were aliens who had been planted here years ago by a UFO. "We came from the level above human in distant space," said a note written by group members before they took their own lives with a combination of alcohol, drugs and suffocation. The timing of their deaths was connected to the appearance in the sky of the spectacular Hale-Bopp comet. Heaven's Gate members believed that a "spacecraft from the Level Above Human" was positioned behind the comet and would swoosh down to pick them up and transport them to their true cosmic home.

There are not enough pages in this book to explore the Japanese cult that released deadly sarin gas into that country's subway system; or the European Solar Temple group which says that suicide can bring rebirth, and which has seen 74 of its members take their own lives between 1994 and 1998. But certainly, not even thirsty old Johnny DoRight would attempt to quench his spiritual thirst with any of these poisonous elixirs.

Jesus warned us about the explosion of deadly religions and false Christ figures nearly 2,000 years ago:

> "If anyone says to you, 'Look, here is the Christ!' or, 'There he is!' do not believe it. For false Christs and false prophets will appear and perform great signs and miracles to deceive even the elect" (Matthew 24:23,24).

A Religious Revolution
It's not just strange new cults that are attracting millions of people today. Mary Rourke, a reporter for the *Los Angeles Times*, wrote that "the United States is experiencing its most dramatic religious transformation in this century" as people raised in Judeo-Christian traditions are becoming Muslims, Hindus, Sikhs or members of other faiths. As a result, writes Rourke, America "is fast becoming the most spiritually diverse country in the world."[5]

Buddhism is an ancient Eastern religious tradition that has become one of the fastest growing faiths in America. Thanks to bands like the Beastie Boys, TV sitcoms like "Dharma and Greg" and movies like *Seven Years in Tibet*, about a selfish man who learns about life from the Dalai Lama, Americans are hearing more about

Buddhism than ever before, and many like what they hear.

The so-called New Age movement isn't as ancient as Buddhism, and sometimes it's difficult to nail down exactly what it is. But it's easy to understand what this large and diverse movement has to offer its disciples. As Erica Goode, a writer for *U.S. News & World Report* put it, the New Age movement represents "a yearning and a search familiar to millions of Americans" and offers "a collection of religious practices, therapy techniques, witchcraft, science fiction and alternative medicine."[6]

As we have seen, New Age spirituality appeals to those who have abandoned more traditional religious faiths. Writes Goode:

> For a generation of lapsed Catholics, Protestants and Jews, the do-it-yourself aspect of self-knowledge is an attractive alternative to organized religion. The pursuit of enlighten-ment needs no intermediaries, no tedious Sunday sermons, no church socials or collection plates. There is no hierarchy, no central religious figure.[7]

Another fast-growing religious fad is the popularity of tele-phone psychics. Even though the well-known Psychic Friends Network has filed for bankruptcy, there are scores of other dial-a-psychic companies filling the void, including Psychic Director Network, Psychic Hotline, Psychic Mystic Network, Psychic Dateline Network, Psychic Health Network, and Psychic Power, to name just a few. Few people realize that psychic practices are con-demned by the Bible, or that many of these phone lines are little more than converted sex phone lines that switched their business to avoid prosecution. People pay 99 cents a minute (or in some cases, $4.99 a minute) to get some reassuring words over the phone from a stranger.

One of the more interesting recent trends has been America's infatuation with angels. Angels seem to be showing up everywhere. They even have their own prime-time TV program, a popular drama in which they appear as human. Most people seem to think of angels as cuddly little supernatural pals who can now be found on lapel pins, stationery, greeting cards, car fresheners and many other incarnations.

You may be asking, *What's wrong with all that, Steve?* As I said earlier in this chapter, I believe the widespread spiritual hunger we are all witnessing today is God-given. At the same time, I believe that many people are looking for God in all the wrong places. And when it comes to finding God, there is really only one place to look. Listen to what Jesus said: "I am the way and the truth and the life. No one comes to the Father except through me" (John 14:6).

Could this be any clearer?

KNOWLEDGE OR IGNORANCE?

Sometimes I'm amazed when I think of everything men and women have been able to accomplish and learn. Take the Internet, for example. I still think it's pretty fabulous that computers can do everything they can do, and the idea of linking computers in a network of communication seems awesome. If you're my age or older, some of the online stuff may baffle you, but check out school-age kids. They can go online, download material they need for research papers, and trade messages with friends down the street or people on the other side of the world whom they have never met. (Unfortunately, some of them also download pornographic photos, which have never before been so easy to access.)

Think about all the knowledge people have amassed about health and nutrition. It's gone way beyond the simple triangle showing the three basic food groups. Now nutritionists know more about the compounds found in hundreds of different foods. And there has been an explosion of new drugs and substances that can be used to treat—and in some cases heal—a whole range of diseases and illnesses.

In recent years human beings have developed tiny cameras that can go into the human body and show us what things look like inside the heart, and they have developed huge telescopes that can help us look into the darkest recesses of our universe. Human beings have explored the bottom of the ocean and the surface of the moon. We have developed new technologies that help doctors perform surgeries that were impossible only a few years ago, and we've also invented new weapons and bombs that carry more destructive power than anyone has ever seen before.

Many of you reading this book right now are extremely knowledgeable about many things, but how much do you know about God? Sadly, I feel that many of us fall miserably short in our knowledge of God. We suffer from the shame of ignorance.

Many of you probably know much more than I do about many, many things, but that's OK. I know a few really important things really well, and I try to act on what I know. I like what Paul said to the believers at Corinth, a city known for the high value it placed on education and learning:

> When I came to you, brothers, I did not come with eloquence or superior wisdom as I proclaimed to you the testimony about God. For I resolved to know nothing while I was with you except Jesus Christ and him crucified. I came to you in weakness and fear, and with much trembling. My message and my preaching were not with wise and persuasive words, but with a demonstration of the Spirit's power, so that your faith might not rest on men's wisdom, but on God's power (1 Corinthians 2:1-5).

Human knowledge used to double every few centuries or so. Then all the knowledge humans had stored in books and papers began to double every generation. Now it is thought that it only takes five years for information to double, and some might even say it's closer to every three to four years. Computers and the Internet give us the kind of access to information that previous generations never dreamed of. Have we all become wiser and better people for it? Do we know the difference between data and wisdom, between information and truth?

LAST DAYS REVIVALS

The following passage sounds like it could be a description of an episode of one of TV's many raucous talk shows. But it was actually written centuries ago, even though it sounds astoundingly contemporary:

> There will be terrible times in the last days. People will be lovers of themselves, lovers of money, boastful, proud, abusive, disobedient to their parents, ungrateful, unholy, without love, unforgiving, slanderous, without self-control, brutal, not lovers of the good, treacherous, rash, conceited, lovers of pleasure rather than lovers of God—having a form of godliness but denying its power. Have nothing to do with them (2 Timothy 3:1-5).

Some people think we are currently in the last days that Paul spoke about when he was writing to his disciple and student, Timothy. There have always been a few folks in every age who thought they would witness the end of human history. It hasn't happened yet, and Jesus even commanded His followers not to be worried about times and dates, but that hasn't slowed down the rush to millennial predictions, a pastime that has even become more popular in the years surrounding 2000.

We may be in the last days (I personally believe we are), or we may have some time left. I don't know, and God hasn't revealed it to me. But as I look around, I see two opposing forces that indicate the time could be growing short. I call those two forces the sin revival and the Holy Ghost revival.

The sin revival is what we read about in our daily newspapers and see on the evening news. For example, American teenagers commit more than 4,000 murders a year. And in places like Jonesboro, Arkansas; Pearl, Mississippi; and Littleton, Colorado, teens turn guns on other teens, shooting at and killing some of their schoolmates. In Paducah, Kentucky, the shooter—Michael Carneal—was only fourteen years old. Three young girls died in that horrible 1997 episode. At the same time, juvenile arrests for serious crimes (we're not talking about stealing gumballs here) are rising to more than 130,000 per year—a 55 percent increase over the last decade.[8]

A few months before ABC's news show "20/20" did a segment on the Brownsville revival, they did a report called *The Heroin Epidemic in America*. Many people thought the drug problem had been settled, but young people seem to be getting more deeply involved in addictive drugs. And other young people regularly engage in a dangerous practice known as "binge drinking." Did you know that according to the National Clearinghouse for Alcohol and Drug Information, over 500,000 people began smoking marijuana for the first time in the first quarter of 1999? Almost one million people began drinking alcohol, and over 200,000 started using hallucinogens in that same period. This speaks of a sweeping sin revival.

I could cite hundreds of other dreadful facts, but I think Bill Bright, founder of Campus Crusade for Christ, clearly summarizes some of our most troublesome current problems in this powerful passage:

> Crime, abortion, divorce, violence, suicide, drug addiction, alcoholism, teen pregnancy, lust, pornography, fornication, adultery, and sodomy run rampant.
>
> Airwaves carry sordid sex into the living room. Condoms are distributed to our children in the public schools. Militant homosexuals parade half-naked down the streets of our nation's capital, demanding approval and special rights as a minority.

America is slaughtering tens of millions of its unborn babies in the womb and arresting those who try to peacefully stop the bloodshed.

Officials have fought vigorously to expel God from our schools. The Ten Commandments cannot even be placed on the walls of most classrooms.

Powerful forces within our country want to make it illegal to mention the name of Jesus, carry Bibles, display religious pictures, or wear Christian emblems in schools and in the workplace. They argue that to do so creates an "offensive environment of harassment."

As a nation, we have spent our way into a $3 trillion national debt. It is still climbing at an alarming rate, threatening to bankrupt our nation in the next few years.

In many instances, our state and local governments are accused of linking arms with organized crime by legalizing lotteries and gaming houses. They are joining the ranks of the largest gambling operators in the world.

Selfishness has become a hallmark of the people. Americans are growing more cynical and less compassionate. Their attitudes toward minorities, immigrants, and the poor have hardened.

This sharp decline into decadence can be traced back to the day when secular humanism began to take control of our country. The level of America's sins would have astounded even ancient Rome whose own moral decay resulted in her self-destruction.[9]

But things aren't all doom and gloom. In fact, this passage was taken from Bright's book, *The Coming Revival*, which argues that God is getting ready to do something amazing in our midst. I believe that by preaching in the Brownsville revival, a Holy Ghost revival full of God's saving and healing miracles, I have been able to participate in part of what God is doing to bring people back to Him.

God has brought renewal to His people during some of the most difficult periods of history. In the Old Testament, King Josiah of Judah restored righteousness to Israel, and the prophets Ezra and Nehemiah helped restore the holy city of Jerusalem. Down through the ages, God has given the world people like Martin Luther and John Wesley—believers who were sold out to Him and helped transform the Church. In American history, there have been at least two major Great Awakenings, as well as many other important renewal movements, including the Azusa Street revivals of the early twentieth century, which helped spark today's worldwide Pentecostal and charismatic movement.

Some might question whether the Brownsville revival is part of God's plan for ushering in the last days, but I do know that people are coming here, meeting God in a powerful way and leaving with a burning passion to love Him and serve Him. God is taking the junk out of their lives and turning them around.

As for me, I'm preaching as if the days were short, and perhaps it would make sense for you to live your life as if your days were numbered, rather than relaxing in the thought that the current good times will never end.

WHICH CAVE ARE YOU IN?

In late September of 1997, *TIME* magazine reported on the death of Shoichi Yokoi. Perhaps you have never heard of this man, but he was a loyal Japanese soldier who hid in the jungles of Guam for decades after World War II had ended.

Nobody had ever seen Yokoi. Whenever he saw anyone nearby, he hid in caves, and he never went shopping for food or clothing. Instead, he ate the plants and animals of the jungle and made his own clothing from tree bark fibers.

U.S. planes had dropped leaflets in the jungle announcing the war's end, but Yokoi suspected foul play and never turned himself in. So from 1945 until 1972—when he was "rescued" by some hunters—he honored the pledge he had made to never surrender.

Sometimes when I think about Yokoi's story, it sounds an awful lot like some of the people I have known. They're out all alone in a big, confusing world. They're still fighting battles that ended years ago. They're running away from the very people who could help them. And they're ignoring important information that could give them the truth about their situation.

Friend, God is trying to get an important message through to you right now. Here's what part of that message says:

I love you. I created you. And that hunger you feel deep inside for truth and wholeness is something I planted within you to lead you to Me. Your hunger won't be filled by false faiths or fleeting pleasures. Only I can complete you. Will you come to Me and give Me your life?

Notes

1. *Emerging Trends,* no. 4 (April 1997), p. 19.
2. Gallup poll, sponsored by CNN, *U.S.A. Today,* conducted by telephone December 16 to 18, 1994.
3. Boy George, *Daily Mail,* (June 1997).
4. Walter Martin, *The Cult Explosion,* New Liberty Videos.
5. Mary Rourke, "Religious Diversity Blooms Big in U.S.," *Pensacola News Journal,* June 24, 1998.
6. Erica Goode, *U.S. News & World Report* (April 7, 1997), p. 32.
7. Ibid.
8. Tom Morganthen, "The Lull Before the Storm," *Newsweek,* December 4, 1995.
9. Bill Bright, *The Coming Revival* (Orlando: New Life Publications, 1995), n.p.

CAN'T BUY ME LOVE

We all want love, but we want it on our own terms.
When it comes to loving God or even
another human being, we must accept no
substitutes for the real thing.

When my wife and I get into the car and drive to the grocery store, it doesn't take a neurosurgeon to know which direction we're going to go. We don't drive the "scenic" route; we take the most direct road there and back.

When a professional baseball player goes up to the plate to bat, we don't have to guess wildly about what he will do. We have tons of statistics that tell us what he has done in the past against left-handed pitchers, against right-handers, when there are men on base or when there are two men out.

I'm a preacher. I tell people about Jesus. That's what I do, and I've been doing it for decades. My years of ministerial experience, including my study of Paul's sermon on Mars Hill in Acts 17, have shown me that people usually respond to a preacher's message in one of three ways.

First there are the *mockers*. These are people who don't want to hear what I'm saying, or they're uncomfortable with it, so they tear it down and make fun of everything I say. Mockers can pick on anything. One may not like my voice; another doesn't like the Bible version I use. To one, I'm too bold; to another I'm not preaching it exactly how they want it. I don't mind it when people have a problem with me, because I'm not a perfect person. But when they make fun of God's message, that troubles me. When they do that, mockers are walking on thin ice.

Next there are the *hesitaters*. These are people who say, "You know, Steve, I'm intrigued by what you're saying. You've got some very interesting points there. I think I'll come back and hear you again tomorrow, or next week, or next year." Sometimes they come back, but most often I never see them again. Instead, they drift off to something else they find interesting.

And finally there are the *responders*. These are the folks who say, "Steve, I may not be sure about you, or your Bible version, but the things you're saying about God make a lot of sense to me, and I'm going to do what you say. I'm going to turn to Jesus." (By the way, all three of these responses can be found at the conclusion of Paul's sermon recorded in Acts 17. We'll talk more about that later.)

I hope you can respond to the things I say in this chapter, because they are extremely important. They are also hard things. What do I mean by that? If I say, "God is love," that's a soft thing. Just about everyone can agree with that. It makes us comfortable. But if I say, "God is a righteous judge who weighs our lives in the balance," that's a hard thing. It makes some people uncomfortable.

I don't like making people uncomfortable, but I do believe in truth in advertising. You're reading this book called *Knockin' at Heaven's Door*. The title speaks of what a lot of people are doing. But I've got news for you: Heaven's door isn't going to open to everyone.

Were you around in April 1964, when the Beatles' song "Can't Buy Me Love" was number one in America? I'm here to tell you that the Beatles were right. Sure, they were speaking of romantic love, but the same principle rings true in the spiritual realm. You can't buy, beg or sneak your way into heaven. There's no way for you to earn God's love. That may seem like bad news, but it's only bad for you if you mock it or hesitate to act on it.

My prayer is that you think about the things we will explore in this chapter. Don't be a mocker or a hesitater. Listen to what God has to say to you, and believe it. If you do that, the door of heaven will open wide for you.

BAD NEWS FOR MODERN MAN

I remember back in the 1970s when the American Bible Society came out with a new, easy-to-read version of the New Testament called *Good News for Modern Man*. This was a very popular Bible, particularly for people like me who were coming to Christ and wanted to read a Bible they could understand. In fact, the term *gospel* means "good news."

But the gospel isn't good news for everybody; just for those who accept it, believe it and live it. Here's what I mean:

Suppose I want to throw a big birthday party for my wife. I can begin by mailing out invitations to her close friends. These invitations spell out where and when the party will be held, what people have to bring and maybe even what they should wear. I might even call some of them on the telephone to remind them about the party, and to tell them how much we would like to see them there.

On the night of the big party, some folks don't show up. One woman may be out of town on business. Another is away visiting friends. Another may want to stay at home and watch the latest episode of her favorite TV sitcom instead of honoring my wife on her birthday.

It's their choice. I have organized the party. I have sent out the invitations. But I can't make people come if they don't want to.

It's the same way with God and heaven. God wants us all to go to heaven. But since He's not a divine dictator, and since we're not all robots following His every command, we can make up our own minds about whether we want to go to heaven or not. God has sent us invitations. For centuries He has told us all about heaven and how to get there. He has sent us His Son to escort us in. He has even given us Jesus' righteousness to clothe our sinful nakedness. But He doesn't force us to enter.

Jesus came to earth to teach us, to die for us and to take our sin on His shoulders. But still, not all of us are going to be able to

GOD IS PLANNING THE BIGGEST PARTY THE UNIVERSE HAS EVER SEEN, BUT SOME OF US AREN'T RESPONDING TO THE INVITATION.

receive His gifts. In fact, some religious folks who thought they were "in" are going to realize they are really "out." Listen to these hard words Jesus has for us:

> "Not everyone who says to me, 'Lord, Lord,' will enter the kingdom of heaven, but only he who does the will of my Father who is in heaven. Many will say to me on that day, 'Lord, Lord, did we not prophesy in your name, and in your name drive out demons and perform many miracles?' Then I will tell them plainly, 'I never knew you. Away from me, you evildoers!' " (Matthew 7:21-23)

Heaven is open, my friend, but not everyone will enter. God is planning the biggest party the universe has ever seen, but some of us aren't responding to the invitation. How about you? Wouldn't you like to be among those who enter in to all God has for us, both then and now?

OUR NEW NUMBER-ONE COMMANDMENT

When Moses climbed Mt. Sinai to receive the Ten Commandments from God, the first commandment was crystal clear: "You shall have no other gods before me" (Exodus 20:3). But many people I have known over the years have created their own number-one commandment. Some have even made this new commandment into a kind of personal god, which they honor and obey before the God of heaven. This new commandment reads like this: "DO YOUR BEST"; it is just part of something we can call "the gospel of achievement."

This commandment is nearly omnipresent. We hear it proclaimed almost everywhere. Before a child takes a test at school, the teacher says, "Do your best." When a coach gathers his players in the locker room for a pep talk, he gives them these final words of advice: "Do your best." When mom and dad drop their son or daughter off at college, they may utter these parting words: "We've worked hard to enable you to be here. Now it's up to you. Do your best." This is the gospel of achievement.

There are two people I immediately think of when I hear that "commandment." For now, I will call them Billy and Sally. Perhaps their stories sound familiar to you.

Billy's Report Card

From the day he was born until the day he went off to school, the words "Do your best" echoed in Billy's ears. His parents were high achievers. They wanted the best for themselves, and they demanded the best of Billy, too.

Whether the setting was kindergarten playtime or his first experiences in reading, writing and arithmetic, Billy was always encouraged to jump higher, read quicker, write better and add faster. And his report cards recorded his achievements. He rarely got lower than an A, and when he did get something lower, he was sure to hear about it.

In the fourth grade, Billy participated in a school spelling bee. He correctly spelled "interrogation" and won the first-place prize, enabling him to go on and compete in a citywide spelling bee. In sixth grade, his science project on photosynthesis won the first-place prize, and he went on to compete in a regional science fair.

By junior high, he was always on the honor roll and had perfect attendance. He was his high school senior class valedictorian. He delivered a speech at his graduation ceremony, and in it he tried to challenge his fellow students to do their best. "We are about to enter the real world," he said. "Second best won't cut it." After graduation, Billy decided he would be a dentist, like his father.

He applied to one of the nation's most prestigious schools of dentistry, and out of the 1,200-plus students who had applied, he was one of the fortunate 85 to be admitted to the program. And what a tough program it was! He routinely canceled the few social engagements he had so he could study late into the night and often into the early morning hours.

His hard work paid off. He graduated with honors and set up his own private practice back home. Now, when he's not with his patients, he's off at a seminar about the latest advances in tooth care technology. He was the first dentist in town to offer laser cleaning and mercury-free fillings.

Billy now has a pretty wife, a big house, two cars, a huge home entertainment center, a dog and a cute little son named Billy Jr. who is just starting kindergarten. And in the mornings, after gulping down some coffee, grabbing his car keys and getting ready to rush off to the office, Billy looks down at Billy Jr. and tells him, "Son, do your best at school today, OK?"

Sally's High Jump

From the time she was four years old, Sally could run like the wind. Her mother—a celebrated high school track star who had received a college athletic scholarship, but had injured herself during her sophomore year—encouraged Sally to exercise, stay away from sweets and fatty foods, and above all else, to do her best.

When she was five, Sally sat glued to the TV set during the Olympics. Inspired by the athletes she saw competing, and amazed by all the attention they received, Sally began pushing herself even harder. In junior high, she began competing in track meets, and when she wasn't competing she was working out. Her friends would invite her to parties, but Sally rarely went. She had to be out on the track early in the morning and didn't want any late-night social activities interfering with her relentless physical regimen.

Her friends had posters of movie stars and rock musicians on their walls, but Sally's walls were decorated with posters of Mary Lou Retton, Florence Griffith Joyner and other top female athletes.

In high school, the hard work began to pay off. Sally broke nearly every school record. She won a college scholarship and was even named one of the NCAA's top women athletes two years in a row. This enabled Sally to travel and speak at school assemblies and track camps. She always closed her speeches with her personal motto, "All you can do is give your very best."

During her junior year in college, Sally competed for a spot on the U.S. Olympic track team in the high jump. But on her final jump, she knocked down the crossbar and was disqualified. Although she told herself she had done her best, she was heartbroken. She ran the next year, back at college, but the thrill was gone. Now younger runners were starting to break the records she had once set.

The Gospel of Achievement: Home Edition

Entire industries have been created to do nothing more than instruct us how to "do our best." Ann Landers's advice appears in hundreds of newspapers, and she's far from the only guru giving advice today. Even more successful is Martha Stewart, the goddess of what she calls "good living." You could work all your life and you would never have a house, a garden or desserts that look as perfect as Martha's, but she earns millions of dollars every year telling us how to try.

I know many parents who instead of really caring for and raising their children merely shower them with gifts and gadgets. Our parents, or grandparents, may have survived the hardships of the Great Depression, but we can hardly survive for a moment without indulging in our creature comforts. As writer Richard Rodriguez puts it:

> My generation, the baby boom generation, was the refoliation of the world. We were the children of mothers who learned how to drive, dyed their hair, used Maybelline, and decorated their houses for Christmas against the knowledge that winter holds sway in the world. Fathers, having returned from blackened theaters of war, used FHA loans to move into tract houses that had no genealogy. In such suburbs, our disillusioned parents intended to ensure their children's optimism.[1]

On the home front, "do your best" often translates into "buy the best," and this endless quest for the best VCR, the most powerful vacuum cleaner, the newest minivan often leads parents to spend more time at work and spend less time with each other or with their kids. Many such overworked relationships end up in divorce, which has a disastrous effect on the family. And what can a guilt-ridden single parent do? Buy more stuff for the kids, that's what!

Is it any wonder so many young people hop into bed with the nearest available partner? Their hunger for true love is so deep that they will take a chance on anything that looks even remotely like love. Is it any surprise that so many young people drink or do drugs? Their pain is so strong that they will try anything to deaden it. Is it surprising to see young people spending hour after hour watching TV, listening to music or cruising the Internet? Their real lives are so sad and lonely that the media's prefabricated virtual lives seem much more interesting.

The Beatles were right. Money can't buy you love.

The Gospel of Achievement: Church Edition

Unfortunately, people often hear the gospel of achievement at church. Sometimes, sermons make it sound like doing good deeds is the surest way to get to heaven. If sermons don't say so, church workers looking for willing volunteers just might.

You've got to help the poor and the needy; serve in the local soup kitchen; deliver dinners to shut-ins on Thanksgiving; ring the bell for Salvation Army around Christmas time; give your tax-deductible gift to the United Way; donate blood to the hospital blood bank; hammer some nails for Habitat for Humanity; and put an extra amount in the offering plate for missionaries, disaster relief funds and church building campaigns.

Don't get me wrong, I'm not against doing good. Jesus commands us to do things like this (see Matthew 25: 35-46); and James tells us that "faith without works is dead" (James 2:26, *KJV*). There's not a church in the world that could survive for long without the work of God-fearing members, and the Brownsville revival depends on the help we receive from hundreds of hardworking volunteers. The members of Brownsville Assembly of God also operate a community outreach program that delivers food, clothes and the gospel to those in need.

What concerns me is when people make it sound like good deeds are some kind of sure-fire way for us to sneak into heaven behind God's back. It's an orientation that starts early, when children who memorize more Bible verses in Sunday School are rewarded more than those who memorize fewer verses, or kids who sing in the choir are believed to be more godly than those who don't.

Every church has its own unique opportunities for each of us to "do our best." I grew up in the Lutheran Church, where being an acolyte was a major milestone during my youth. In the Catholic church down the street, attending mass, saying prayers and going to confession were essential. For Mormons, going overseas for two years of missionary work is a prerequisite for entry into heaven. And for Jehovah's Witnesses, attending frequent Bible studies, knocking on doors and handing out copies of *Watchtower* bring eternal rewards.

I haven't mentioned Pentecostals yet, but they have their own ways of preaching the message of "do your best." For us, that involves being more filled with the Spirit than everyone else, speaking in tongues more or having more prophecies, or praying longer, singing louder or even occupying an important spot in the church choir's annual singing Christmas tree extravaganza.

YOU CAN GO TO HELL WITH BAPTISMAL WATERS ON YOUR FACE; YOU CAN GO TO HELL WITH A CHOIR ROBE ON; YOU CAN GO TO HELL WITH A COMMUNION CUP IN YOUR HAND AND A WAFER IN YOUR MOUTH. NOT ONE OF THEM WILL GET YOU TO HEAVEN.

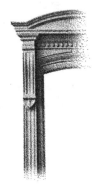

Much of the time, most of this so-called religious behavior is really nothing more than a confused attempt to impress our friends and, if we're lucky, impress God, too. But God is not impressed. Listen to Jesus' words to those who publicly parade their religiosity:

> Be careful not to do your "acts of righteousness" before men, to be seen by them. If you do, you will have no reward from your Father in heaven.
> So when you give to the needy, do not announce it with trumpets, as the hypocrites do...
> And when you pray, do not be like the hypocrites, for

they love to pray standing in the synagogues and on the street corners to be seen by men (Matthew 6:1,2,5).

Anyone who has ever attended the Brownsville revival has heard me say: You can go to hell with baptismal waters on your face, you can go to hell with a choir robe on, you can go to hell with a communion cup in your hand and a wafer in your mouth. Friend, all these things are good, but not one of them will get you to heaven.

WHEN DOING YOUR BEST JUST ISN'T GOOD ENOUGH

Once when Jesus was out walking and teaching among the people, He was approached by a man who had "done his best" from the time he was an infant, and had grown very wealthy in the process. The man asked Jesus a simple question: "Teacher, what good thing must I do to get eternal life?"

Jesus looked the man in the eye (and, I believe, looked into his very soul) and gave a surprising answer. Let's read about the encounter as Matthew recorded it:

Jesus answered, "If you want to be perfect, go, sell your possessions and give to the poor, and you will have treasure in heaven. Then come, follow me."

When the young man heard this, he went away sad, because he had great wealth.

After a few moments, Jesus' confused disciples—Matthew says they were "greatly astonished"—looked at Him and asked Him this question: "Who then can be saved?"

Jesus looked at them and said, "With man this is impossible, but with God all things are possible" (see Matthew 19:16-26).

The man had thought that the doors of heaven would be wide open for him. After all, through most of his life he had rarely encountered closed doors in anything he had attempted. But the cost of following Jesus was simply too much for him to bear. Jesus didn't want the man's résumé or lifetime list of impressive achievements, He wanted his heart. Unfortunately, the man's heart was set on other things.

The door of heaven will open, my friend, but only to those who are willing to enter God's way. Our own achievements, even our own superreligiosity, mean less than nothing to God. Here's how Isaiah stated this:

> All of us have become like one who is unclean, and all our righteous acts are like filthy rags (Isaiah 64:6).

Or as Paul told Titus:

> [God] saved us, not because of righteous things we had done, but because of his mercy. He saved us through the washing of rebirth and renewal by the Holy Spirit (Titus 3:5).

Remember our two achievers Billy and Sally? They spent their lives doing their best. But remember, when it comes to your personal salvation, even your best won't do. Only the precious blood of Jesus can wash away your sins and open the door of heaven for you.

Most people are certain they are going to heaven, but I'm afraid that many of these folks are in for the shock of their lives. They will stand before God, waiting to hear the words, "Come on in!" but instead they will hear God shout out, "Go away! I never knew you."

I pray that you won't be among them.

Notes

1. Richard Rodriguez, *U.S. News & World Report* (April 7, 1997), p. 62.

chapter

6

TRICKLE-DOWN TROUBLE

One thing usually leads to another.
But when it comes to our own moral compromises
and failures, our problems have a bad
influence on others.

I love my children, and I do my best to be a good dad. But I'm not perfect. I learned this the hard way when something that should have been a fun little shopping trip turned into a nightmare.

My family and I were in London. We had a few days off from our ministry responsibilities and decided to go to Harrod's, which is one of the world's most famous department stores. My wife wanted to look at women's clothing, and I wanted to go to the men's department, which was on another floor. So we split up, agreeing that I would take our son Ryan, who was about four years old at the time.

"I'll keep an eye on him, honey," I said. And that's what I did, at least for a while.

I remember walking over to look at a number of racks of shirts. I would sort through a few shirts, then look down at Ryan, who was standing right there next to me. So far so good.

I grabbed Ryan's hand and headed for the suit department. I was fascinated with their vast selection. Ryan stuck by my side as I checked out a line of sport coats.

Then it happened. I found myself hovering over a table of neck-ties and got a little bit sidetracked by all the colorful designs. When I looked down to check on Ryan, he was nowhere in sight.

If you're a parent, you know exactly what I was feeling at that moment. I was utterly panic-stricken. All I could see were hundreds and hundreds of unfamiliar faces surrounding me, moving in a thousand different directions and calling out to each other in loud voices. The scene was utter chaos.

I'm not a paranoid person, but I felt a wave of fear pass over me. Perhaps someone had taken him. London is a big city full of near-ly nine million people. Who knows who might have been in the store that day?

I raced through Harrod's, which if you've ever seen it is an amazingly huge store. I ran from one department to another, call-ing out, "Ryan! Ryan!" It seemed like I had been searching for hours, but after what was really just a couple of intense minutes, I heard a stern response.

"Are you looking for a small boy in a red jacket?" a uniformed man asked me.

"Yes!" I responded. The security officer then ushered me to another floor where Ryan was being protected and watched over by Harrod's helpful staff. Ryan hadn't disappeared forever, he had merely walked to another part of the store.

I've often thought about that day since then. That simple little trip to the store could have been tragic. If something bad had hap-pened to Ryan, it would have been my fault.

I fail as a dad sometimes. In some cases, my failures are silly and have little impact. Other times, they are much more serious. Either way, it's amazing to me how much I influence my son, even when I'm not intending to.

I like joking around with Ryan. One day I bent my index finger over at the knuckle, and put the knuckle up against my nose so it looked like I was picking my nose. You may think that's gross or immature, but Ryan thought it was pretty funny. It wouldn't have been so funny, though, if the next day Ryan had imitated his dad's trick at school and got sent home for making a scene. This would have been what I call trickle-down trouble.

On a more serious note, I once endangered Ryan's life by speeding around our property on one of those Yamaha four-wheelers that are so much fun to ride. I've been driving cars and motorcycles for decades, so I occasionally drive the Yamaha faster than a child should drive it. But one day I was shocked to see Ryan get on the four-wheeler, rev it up and head at full speed for a bump. The next thing I knew, Ryan and the machine were flying through the air like he was some kind of circus stunt rider. That was trickle-down trouble, too.

Ryan scared me to death. He even scared himself a little. And after that thrill ride, Ryan and I sat down and had a long talk about responsible driving.

I'll never forget what the American-born writer James Baldwin said: "Children never have been very good at listening to their elders, but they have never failed to imitate them."

LOVING THE LITTLE ONES

There's a beautiful passage in the Gospel of Matthew that shows us Jesus' love for children, as well as His love for the childlike part all of us have deep down inside.

Sometimes Jesus would walk among the crowds and teach. At other times, He would speak privately to His disciples. Some of the things He spoke to His disciples during these private times together were among the most powerful things He ever said.

One day, when they were all together, the disciples asked Him, "Who is the greatest in the kingdom of heaven?" Jesus called a little child to His side and gave the disciples this startling answer:

"I tell you the truth, unless you change and become like little children, you will never enter the kingdom of heaven. Therefore, whoever humbles himself like this child is the greatest in the kingdom of heaven. And whoever welcomes a little child like this in my name welcomes me" (Matthew 18:3-5).

But then, as He often did, Jesus gave His disciples the answer to a question they hadn't even asked:

"But if anyone causes one of these little ones who believe in me to sin, it would be better for him to have a large millstone hung around his neck and to be drowned in the depths of the sea" (verse 6).

To you, these may sound like harsh words from Jesus. But I think they're right on. The world is full of people who live their lives as if their behavior had no impact on anyone else. They may just be trying to get by, trying to survive another day, but they leave a trail of destruction behind them.

The first major crime recorded in the Bible is in Genesis chapter four, where Cain murders his brother Abel. God came along later and asked Cain where Abel was. Cain's response has become the motto of all those who avoid responsibility: "Am I my brother's keeper?" (Genesis 4:9).

God's answer to that question, my friend, is a straightforward, unambiguous yes. Our behavior can influence other people. Our sin and deceit can close the door of heaven for others, preventing them from entering in. This is why Jesus tells His disciples that those who cause an innocent one to sin would have been better off drowning in the ocean depths. God doesn't like our trickle-down trouble.

THE LAW OF UNINTENDED CONSEQUENCES

I don't know if you've ever witnessed how a chain-reaction highway accident begins, but it usually happens like this: Joe Speed Demon is putting the pedal to the metal in his souped-up Mustang, rapidly weaving in and out of each and every lane of traffic. His behavior requires Joanne Soccer Mom to step on her brakes so she can keep her minivan from running into Joe during one of his sudden lane changes. Joanne's braking requires the elderly couple behind her to brake, too. That's the way it continues to go until some poor soul chooses the wrong moment to reach down to adjust the car radio or flick an ash off of his cigarette, and he looks up to find himself hurtling toward the back of the car in front of him. Within seconds, cars are crashing into one another like a toppled row of strategically placed dominoes.

Joe Speed Demon never really intended to hurt anyone. He may not even be aware that he caused a multicar pileup. But every year, irresponsible drivers like him cause hundreds of accidents, injuries and deaths on America's highways.

I loved my dad, but some of his own trouble unintentionally trickled down to me, and it caused me a world of hurt.

My dad was a military man. I used to enjoy hearing him talk about his actions in World War II, and looking at his military memorabilia. My favorite item was his genuine Japanese sword. His stories never failed to captivate me. He was a great man.

But he was also an avid beer drinker. Every night after work, he would come home, sit down in his big, comfy chair and start tossing down a Falstaff or Schlitz. About the time I was eight, at my request, he began pouring me little glasses of beer.

My dad certainly had no intention of turning me into an alcoholic. He might not even have been aware that he had a drinking problem himself. I'm not sure. But one thing I do know is that he helped me develop a taste for alcohol at a very early age. By the time I was 12 years old, I was drinking as much as my dad was. I remember paying people to buy me beer with money I had stolen from Dad's wallet or Mom's purse. I believe that by the time I hit 15, I was a full-fledged alcoholic. Talk about unintended consequences! My troubles with alcohol and substance abuse began at my father's side.

Unintended consequences do not hurt only those who are close to us. Sometimes they hurt people we will never meet who are thousands of miles away.

Every month, thousands of men plop down money for the latest copy of *Hustler* magazine or some of the other plentiful pornography that so many people call "adult entertainment." These men will argue that porn doesn't hurt them, but ask their wives. How

GOD DOESN'T WANT US TO BLUNDER THROUGH LIFE LIKE A BULL IN A CHINA SHOP, WREAKING PAIN AND HAVOC WHEREVER WE GO; HE WANTS US TO BE GOOD STEWARDS OF OUR INFLUENCE—SENSITIVE TO THE NEEDS AND VULNERABILITIES OF OTHERS AND SENSITIVE TO HIM.

many men have become sex-obsessed and self-centered, in part because the message of these magazines is that women exist to fulfill their every fantasy?

Others *are* hurt by porn. Pornography is a huge industry that depends on a constant stream of fresh young victims. We've all heard the stories about girls who go to Hollywood looking for a career in show business. But what happens when they can't pay their rent? Some pornographer appears and offers them lots of money for a few hours of work. Where does that money come from? From the men who buy the magazines. They fund an industry that is busy victimizing someone else's young daughter. They are helping to cause an innocent to fall into sin.

God doesn't want us to blunder through life like a bull in a china shop, wreaking pain and havoc wherever we go. He wants us to be good stewards of our influence. He calls us to be sensitive to the needs and vulnerabilities of others and to be sensitive to Him. You may not be teaching your son to drink, or financing a young girl's descent into the seedy world of pornography, but what kind of influence do you have in this world?

Is your influence a good and healthy one? When people are around for a while, do they leave better people, or do they carry your weaknesses away with them? What do the people who live with you or work with you think about your inner person—your character, your personality, your true nature? Do people trust you when they turn their backs on you, or are they wary and cautious? What kind of person are you?

Before moving on, let me say one more thing. I'm sure every citizen of the United States has been saddened by the negative example our commander in chief William Jefferson Clinton set before us. Little children were asking serious questions like, "What's adultery?" or "What did the president do with that woman in his office?" The bottom line is, he set a bad example, and it was one that parents all over America had to explain to their young children.

GOD'S SERENADE

God knows exactly who you are. He ought to know; He created you.

I don't know if you're aware of it or not, but from the beginning of your life, God has been singing a love song to you. God saw you before you even were. He has known you since before you were born. He had a plan for you long before you began thinking about what you wanted to be when you grew up. And He has been singing His love songs to you from the beginning.

God's songs aren't like some of the overly dramatic arias you might hear in Italian operas. Instead, His songs are clear and direct:

"I have loved you with an everlasting love;
I have drawn you with loving-kindness" (Jeremiah 31:3).

"Before I formed you in the womb I knew you,
before you were born I set you apart" (Jeremiah 1:5).

By day the LORD directs his love,
at night his song is with me (Psalm 42:8).

For God so loved the world that he gave his one and only son, that whoever believes in him shall not perish but have eternal life (John 3:16).

These are just some of the wonderful love songs God has been singing to us from the beginning of our lives. From the Cross, Jesus saw your cradle and began wooing you to Himself. From the manger, Jesus saw the danger you would encounter in life and sought to give you protective covering.

Have you heard these songs? Have you returned God's love? It took me a long time to hear and respond. If I had responded to God's love earlier in life, I could have spared myself and a lot of other people a lot of pain.

A LIVING LEGACY

Christianity was introduced to Finland by traders and merchants sometime during the thirteenth century. A few centuries later, reformers influenced by Martin Luther came to Finland, and in time the country became Lutheran. Today, 90 percent of Finns are members of the Evangelical Lutheran Church of Finland, although God only knows how many of these people are devoted followers of Jesus. Still, that's where my mom's side of the family came from. God has been wooing our family for centuries.

I never knew my grandfather, but he was the first person to tell my mama about Jesus. My dad was not a churchgoing man, but Mama has tried to follow Jesus all her life. And from the time I was a tiny child, she tried to get me to follow Him, too.

I remember coloring pictures of Jesus in children's class at the Lutheran church. Mama recently gave me some of these pictures. They are big pictures with only a few words, like "Jesus is good," or "Jesus is kind." I remember being five years old and looking at these pictures and feeling good things about Jesus. He was wooing me then.

Later, in Vacation Bible School, I sang, "Jesus loves me, this I know, for the Bible tells me so." Next, I was in the children's choir. I remember our Lutheran pastor telling Mama, "I'm so proud of Steve! He opens his mouth so wide!" And he meant it as a compliment. God was trying to get ahold of me then.

I heard about how Jesus went to the Cross and died for me. I heard about sin, sacrifice and blood. It didn't make too much sense to me, but they taught these things to me anyway, hoping they would stick somehow.

When I was eight, Billy Graham came to Huntsville to preach at a crusade at Redstone Arsenal. It was 1962, and the Lord was really trying to get ahold of me. I remember Billy Graham preaching, but my heart wasn't in it. Then George Beverly Shea got up and sang, "Just as I am, without one plea." Thousands of people went forward to accept Christ, but I stayed behind.

Years later, when I was hitchhiking across the country, I would think about the gospel message when I went to rescue missions to scrounge something to eat. People would hand me a sandwich and tell me about Jesus. I wasn't ready to believe what they said, but those sandwiches kept me going for another day.

How has God wooed you? Maybe you go to church on Christmas because you know there's something more to Christmas than trees and presents, and while you're there you hear something about the birth of Jesus. Or maybe you go to church on Easter and hear a sermon about the Resurrection. Or maybe the church puts on an Easter cantata, and you find yourself crying there in the dark as people sing beautiful songs about a risen Savior who came to redeem the world.

Maybe you've been out driving late at night, and you tuned in to a preacher's voice on the radio. His accent may have sounded funny, and he may have yelled a bit too much for your liking, but he said something about Jesus dying for you, and it struck a chord in your heart.

The Lord is standing outside your window. He's strumming His guitar. He's singing you His love songs. Are you listening? Or are you drowning it out?

I remember one song I used to listen to that helped me drown out God's loving serenade. It was a song by the Rolling Stones called "Sympathy for the Devil," which included the classic line, "Pleased to meet you, hope you guessed my name." I remember listening to that song when it came out in 1968. In 1999, a 55-year-old Mick Jagger was still singing the song, which served as an encore to the Stones' "No Security" tour. Some things never change, my friend. God is still trying to woo us, and the devil is still trying to drown out God's beautiful love songs.

God Woos the Most Unlikely People

Sometimes God's serenade doesn't get through to people. But other times it does. And it never ceases to amaze me the kinds of people who hear God calling and give Him their lives. Let me tell you the true story of how God wooed a biker dude, a hippie chick and at least half of a church.

A few years ago, when I visited a church out in the West, the pastor tapped me on the arm and said, "See that fellow over there? He's got quite a story."

The story began in the 1970s, during the height of the hippie movement. The pastor was preaching his Sunday sermon to a couple hundred people. At that time, most church folks didn't know what to make of the hippies. So imagine the shock when this big, long-haired, bearded hippie biker, sporting Levi's, tattoos and sunglasses walked in and grabbed a seat in the back pew. He stayed for a while and listened to what the pastor was preaching. Then, before the service was over, he got up and walked out. Nobody said it out loud, but a lot of the congregation felt relieved after the stranger was gone.

The next Sunday he was back, and this time he brought his female counterpart along with him to the little church. She was an exotic-looking woman with blonde hair flowing down to her hips and wearing skintight jeans and a scanty little tie-dyed top. The counterculture couple sat in the back pew where the man had sat alone the previous week. They left before the service ended. The parishioners didn't know what to think. But the pastor prayed, both for the hippie couple and for his church.

The third Sunday, the biker man and the hippie chick were back. But this time they brought a whole entourage with them—almost a dozen lost souls in all. And when the pastor looked at them and gave the invitation, most of them came forward to accept Christ.

The congregation didn't know what to do now. At a divisive church meeting held later that week, church members split right down the middle. Half wanted to welcome the hippies with open arms, but the other half wanted the pastor to find a nice way to politely kick them out. The pastor sided with the open-armers and welcomed the hippies. The other members left and started a new church down the street. The pastor was worried. He thought he was doing what Jesus would have done, but he had just said good-bye to half of his members. In the years that followed, he kept preaching to hippies, to bikers, to baby boomers, to bankers and to anybody else who would listen.

Today that pastor's church has thousands of members, including that original biker, who is now a very successful businessman and one of the church's biggest financial supporters. Just like a lot of drug dealers I used to know, this man became very successful once God got ahold of him and gave him a new direction in life. Now this man isn't selling drugs to kids anymore. Instead, he's having a positive influence on many, many people.

THE SOUL OF A SHEPHERD

A short time after Jesus told His disciples they needed to become like little children to enter the kingdom of heaven, He told them the following story about a man and his sheep:

> "What do you think? If a man owns a hundred sheep, and one of them wanders away, will he not leave the ninety-nine on the hills and go to look for the one that wandered off? And if he finds it, I tell you the truth, he is happier about that one sheep than about the ninety-nine that did not wander off. In the same way, your Father in heaven is not willing that any of these little ones should be lost" (Matthew 18:12-14).

God loves all of us, and that includes those of us who wander off as well as those of us who don't. But He has little patience with those who would attempt to lure the sheep away from the Shepherd's care.

Heed God's call on your life. Respond to His persistent serenade by giving Him your life and your love. And use your influence to do good in the world, spreading His love and light while helping introduce others to the love of God.

chapter

7

WHEN WHAT'S
WRONG IS RIGHT

*People may try to blur the lines
between right and wrong,
but that doesn't change the
unchangeable laws of the universe.
God gave humanity the Ten Commandments,
not the ten suggestions.*

When Moses went up Mt. Sinai to receive God's law, he got the Ten Commandments, not the ten suggestions. "I am the Lord your God," thundered the Almighty, who enumerated a set of commands that are enshrined in the laws of most of the nations on earth:

You shall not murder.

You shall not commit adultery.

You shall not steal.

You shall not give false testimony against your neighbor.

The Ten Commandments aren't personal preferences. They're not the results of a *New York Times* poll. And they're not options. These are unchangeable laws of the universe, not "good ideas" that may work just fine for one person but not for another.

One might think that the Ten Commandments would be honored as God's absolute law by churches throughout the land. But sadly, such is not the case. Pollster George Barna interviewed hundreds of people—including those who call themselves Christians and those who don't—and asked them whether or not they agreed with this simple, straightforward statement: "There is no such thing as absolute truth; different people can decide truth in conflicting ways and still be correct."

Among nonchurchgoers, 81 percent agreed that there is no such thing as absolute truth. That shouldn't surprise us too much. But what shocked me was that among adults associated with mainline Protestant churches (that would be many Methodists, Presbyterians and Lutherans), 73 percent said there were no moral absolutes. And even among evangelicals, who claim to believe in the inspiration and authority of Scripture, around half agree with the statement, "There is no such thing as absolute truth."[1]

This would explain the recent lesbian wedding performed in California by United Methodist clergy. Over 1,200 invited guests were present at the Sacramento Convention Center on January 16, 1999 to witness and bless this union. Even though this type of ceremony is forbidden by the denomination, over 150 clergy members forged ahead. The United Methodist magazine, *Good News,* states that "this act is bringing further division and polarization to our church."[2] This is just an example of the widespread controversy over absolute truth.

QUIET IN THE COURTROOM!

Welcome to the courtroom, ladies and gentlemen. No, this isn't the U.S. Senate chamber, where 100 of America's elected representatives gathered in early 1999 to vote on the fate of impeached President Bill Clinton. And it isn't courtroom TV or even reruns of "Perry Mason." This is the courtroom of God, where before us stand right and wrong.

We are living in truly shocking times. People's values are being tested with an intense, white-hot heat. Morality and goodness are on the witness stand, where they are being cross-examined by a team of high-powered attorneys. You and everyone else are sitting in the courtroom, anxiously awaiting the judge's verdict. Truth hangs in the balance.

What is right and what is wrong? What is good and what is bad? What is moral and what is evil? Is there a set of unchangeable laws and universal rules that tell us what behavior is permissible and what is clearly out of bounds?

What does it mean when someone puts a hand on a Bible and swears to God? It could be a local dogcatcher being sworn in down at the county building with just a few people watching. It could be the nationally televised inauguration of the president of the United States for a new four-year term. Or it could be a man and a woman, standing before hundreds of friends and family members, placing their hands on a Bible together and swearing to love, honor and care for each other "till death do us part."

What if the dogcatcher decides to sleep on the job instead of rounding up rabid animals? Or what if the president violates the oath and ethics of his high office? Or what if the man and woman decide that the grass is greener on the other side and ditch their vows as too confining or inconvenient? Do vows sworn before God mean anything, or can we break them at will?

Is adultery wrong? How about murder? How about stealing? How about lying? Is *anything* really wrong anymore?

Please, ladies and gentlemen. We must have quiet in the courtroom. The trial of the century is about to begin.

Preachers Wanted

Most pastors have job descriptions, and their duties commonly include things like preaching the Sunday sermon, marrying and burying church members, visiting the sick and the elderly and managing the church's finances.

But God Himself is the author of the best pastoral job description ever written. It comes from the pen of Paul and is found in the New Testament. It reads like a solemn inauguration oath for a man or woman of God:

> In the presence of God and of Christ Jesus, who will judge the living and the dead, and in view of his appearing and his kingdom, I give you this charge:
>
> Preach the Word; be prepared in season and out of season; correct, rebuke and encourage—with great patience and careful instruction. For the time will come when men will not put up with sound doctrine. Instead, to suit their own desires, they will gather around them a great number of teachers to say what their itching ears want to hear. They will turn their ears away from the truth and turn aside to myths (2 Timothy 4:1-4).

What a challenging assignment! But it is one I joyfully accept, because it is the calling God has given me. However, there's another important reason I want to preach the Word, and that reason is you.

Just about everybody is looking for God in one way or another, but things don't always turn out as people might hope.

Have you ever attended a backyard barbecue at a home where they have one of those high-tech bug zappers? The zapper radiates light that attract bugs from near and far. The bugs are drawn to the light, then head straight for the zapper, where they are instantly pulverized by an intense burst of electricity.

The same kind of thing happens to many people today. They are hungry for God, but they get off track somewhere along the way. They become seduced by pleasures or riches, or they become ensnared by a false religion or a cult, or they trade the unchangeable laws of God for an ever-changing set of personal moral codes they use for a while before trading them in on a new set.

Heaven is closed to such people, my friend, and it's not because

God has locked them out and barred the door. Rather, they have shut themselves off from knowing God as He is and enjoying all He has to offer us. Or as a wise man named Solomon once put it:

There is a way that seems right to a man,
but in the end it leads to death (Proverbs 14:12).

Don't let yourself get zapped, my friend. Follow the tried and proven path to God. In this chapter, we'll show you how.

Church Shop Until You Drop!

A lot of people are going church shopping today. They're looking for a church that's a perfect fit, with an entertaining and jovial pastor, a top-notch worship band, a comfortable and well-lighted sanctuary, a full range of programming options for everybody in the family and a schedule of weekly services that doesn't crimp anyone's hectic social calendar.

Somewhere out there is a church for everybody. Take the First Presleyterian Church of Elvis the Divine, located in Bethlehem, Pennsylvania. (I'm not kidding. This is a real-life registered church.) The "king" is king indeed at this highly specialized church.

Or if you're in Arizona and want a church that blows your mind, check out the Peyote Way Church of God, where psychedelic drugs promise to escort you to the portals of spiritual power.[3]

If you're gay and you don't want to be bothered by Bible passages critical of your lifestyle, there are many churches around the world that are affiliated with a gay-friendly denomination, the Metropolitan Community Churches. We checked out the website of one of the denomination's biggest congregations, the Metropolitan Community Church of Dallas, and we found a sermon there called "Adam, Steve and Eve."

You don't even have to go to one of these churches to see the homosexual lifestyle receive a glowing endorsement from the pulpit. As we mentioned before, renegade clergy in the Methodist and

Episcopal churches have created controversies by ordaining openly gay couples to the clergy or performing same-sex commitment ceremonies. These pastors' denominations don't approve of what they're doing, but many people say it will just be a matter of time before they do. What would John Wesley, the Bible-preaching revivalist who founded the Methodist church, say about this if he were alive today?

Some "mainstream" denominations are more openly pro-gay than others. In a November 1998 news release, Rev. Paul Sherry, president of the liberal United Church of Christ, said opposition to homosexuality is based on "the assumption, frequently untested, that the Bible in general, and Christianity in particular, teach that homosexuality is a sin." (Memo to Mr. Sherry: please read Romans 1:26,27 and 1 Corinthians 6:9,10.) Instead of taking the Bible at its word about sin, Mr. Sherry wants to create an all-inclusive church that supports "the full inclusion and participation of all God's children."

I have nothing against homosexuals. They are sinners like the rest of us, and some of them aren't as sex-obsessed as some heterosexuals I know. Plus, it was an advocate of the gay lifestyle who was the author of one of the best articles anyone has ever written about the Brownsville revival. It was an article he wrote for *SPIN*, a national music magazine, and it was a fair story.[4] But I do have a problem with teachers who ignore sound doctrine and give people what their itching ears want to hear.

That's exactly what the Ku Klux Klan did. They didn't like what the Bible said about loving our neighbor, so they created a movement and a church that was a nice little club for bigots. Their message was, "Hey, if you hate blacks, Jews or immigrants, come on over and burn a cross with us!" To the hard-core KKK members, burning a cross wasn't a sign of disrespect to Christianity. Rather, they saw it as symbolic of the fire of God's truth. God loves KKK members, racist skinheads, militia members and everyone else. But He condemns their hatred for other people, because God created us all.

Just about everybody seems to have his own image of Jesus.

There is a book written by Bruce Barton called *The Man Nobody Knows*. It was published in 1924. Have you heard of it? To Barton, Jesus was little more than a successful executive. Barton even called Jesus "the founder of modern business."

I'm not sure what Barton did with the passage in Matthew 21 that shows Jesus overturning the tables of the moneychangers and driving the merchants from the temple. Clearly, this was a case of the biblical Jesus contradicting the nonbiblical image someone was trying to create.

Many people imagine Jesus as a nice guy, but Jesus wasn't too nice to people who were twisting the Word of God. Listen to His scathing attack on self-righteous Jewish leaders:

> "Woe to you, teachers of the law and Pharisees, you hypocrites! You shut the kingdom of heaven in men's faces. You yourselves do not enter, nor will you let those enter who are trying to" (Matthew 23:13).

And that's just the beginning of a lengthy barrage of searing rebukes. In the 23 verses that follow, Jesus calls these misguided teachers "blind guides," "blind fools," "whitewashed tombs," "snakes" and a "brood of vipers." So much for Jesus, meek and mild, the imaginary leader of the Church of Anything Goes.

SEEKING REFUGE

I live in southern Alabama, about 30 minutes away from the Gulf of Mexico. I love this area, but there's one thing I don't appreciate too much, and that's the frequent hurricanes that pass through here.

Some years are tougher than others, but 1998 was particularly stormy, thanks in part to Hurricane Georges, which ripped through much of the South. Things were so bad in New Orleans that owners closed down all the bars on Bourbon Street in the historic French Quarter. Still, some folks brought their own booze and strolled down the historic street as the storm howled. "If we die, at least we'll die happy," a 25-year-old California woman told the Associated Press. "Besides, if you're drunk enough, you aren't scared."[5]

Others sought refuge in stable structures like steel-reinforced buildings or, better yet, bomb shelters. Those who sought shelter in flimsy mobile homes or beachfront condos risked exposing themselves to an unplanned but *uplifting* experience!

But it's not just tropical storms that cause people to seek refuge. Sometimes, our inability to face up to our own sinfulness leads some of us to seek refuge from God. The prophet Isaiah calls this search for a place to hide from God a refuge of lies. (See Isaiah 28:15.)

The first recorded case of this evasive behavior is found in the book of Genesis. Adam and Eve have fallen from innocence in the Garden of Eden. In their fallen state, they are suddenly ashamed of their own nakedness, so they decide to hide from God:

> Then the man and his wife heard the sound of the LORD God as he was walking in the garden in the cool of the day, and they hid from the LORD God among the trees of the garden. But the LORD God called to the man, "Where are you?"
>
> He answered, "I heard you in the garden, and I was afraid because I was naked; so I hid" (Genesis 3:8-10).

People have been hiding from God ever since, and in our day it seems their efforts to make themselves scarce take one of the following four forms.

The Refuge of Running

Jonah is probably the best-known biblical example of someone who ran from God. In fact, there's an entire book of the Bible dedicated to his futile efforts to get away from the Almighty.

Jonah hopped on a boat and tried to sail away from the presence of God. But instead of sneaking into the sunset, Jonah found himself in the midst of a Hurricane Georges-size storm which threatened to sink the boat. The men on board realized Jonah was the source of their problems, so they threw him overboard, where he was picked up by a big fish that happened to be passing through the area.

Today we've got all kinds of high-speed transportation devices that Jonah didn't have in his day. Some people may believe that the world's fastest planes, cars or trains can transport them out of the presence of God and away from their own complex problems. But not even the Concorde, a supersonic trans-Atlantic jet that gets you from New York to London in a few hours, can do that.

King David tried to run from God, but realized God was everywhere. Here's how he expressed it in Psalm 139:7,8:

> Where can I go from your Spirit?
> Where can I flee from your presence?
> If I go up to the heavens, you are there;
> If I make my bed in the depths, you are there.

The Refuge of Relationships

Those who get tired of running often settle down into a relationship with another person or with a group.

I wish I had a dollar for every quickie marriage performed in just one of the many wedding chapels that do a brisk business in Las Vegas. While some of these flings may last, many of them represent little more than an ill-fated effort to run from the presence of God and into the arms of a human partner.

Marriage is hard work, my friend. Martin Luther called it "a school for character" because marriage, when it's done the way God wants us to do it, shows us things about ourselves we don't necessarily want to see, forcing us to change and grow up. It will seldom succeed if it is only a refuge for people on the run.

Another form of relationship that some refuge seekers embrace is gangs. Gangs are especially appealing to young people who have grown up in dysfunctional or abusive families, since the gang's tight structure serves as a replacement for the familial love they never experienced. But even though they can provide a needed sense of community and belonging, gangs can never replace the love of God.

The Refuge of Religion

It may surprise you to hear a preacher say that religion is a place where people can run from God, but not all religions are created equal.

Marianne Williamson has made tons of money writing books

RELIGION FEELS GOOD AND MAKES US FEEL LIKE BETTER PEOPLE. CHRISTIANITY HURTS, AND MAKES US SEE HOW WICKED AND SINFUL WE ARE. IT'S NOT ABOUT EXTERNAL THINGS, MY FRIEND, BUT ABOUT THE HEART.

about spirituality. She has even appeared on Oprah Winfrey's TV show, and once she led Oprah's studio audience in something she called "prayer." But Williamson doesn't define prayer the same way the Bible does. She bases her beliefs on a system called a "Course in Miracles," and according to this system, God doesn't really exist, but is just a figment of our fertile imagination. Williamson and the "Course in Miracles" teach us to connect with divinity by "praying" to ourselves. Friend, this kind of spirituality is a dangerous place to hide from God.

You don't even have to go outside of Christianity to find adulterated or watered-down truth. I believe the devil works overtime on Sunday morning, and he's not always working to keep people away from church. Sometimes Satan and his demonic coworkers like to encourage people to go to church, but only for an hour or so, and never with the intention of having people believe in God and follow what He says. By going to church, some people can get their religious itch scratched for a few minutes before going back home and doing what they normally do the rest of the week.

I am convinced more than ever before of my previous statement, "Religion is hanging around the Cross, but Christianity is getting on the Cross." Religion feels good and makes us feel like better people. Christianity hurts, and makes us see how wicked and sinful we are. Also, don't forget what I said in the previous chapter: People can go to hell with a choir robe on and a communion wafer in their mouth. It's not about external things, friend, but about the heart.

The Refuge of Riches

I used to know a woman who was an alcoholic. She would talk to me about God sometimes, but every time I began to get heavy with her about her alcoholism, she would change the subject. And whenever she was falling under really serious conviction about God, she would take a cruise to the Bahamas. A few weeks later I would see her again, and her dependency on drinking would be worse than before. For this woman and millions like her, riches are a crutch that can be used to run from God.

I once met a man who believed that God had called him to serve overseas as a missionary. But as a young man he didn't feel he had enough money to cover his living expenses, so he bought a cheap run-down house and spent the next few months repairing it. He painted the outside, repaired the inside, landscaped the yard and installed new plumbing and fixtures. When he sold the house, he made double what he had invested. He was so excited about his success that he decided he would buy another house and make some more money.

Now it's 25 years—and dozens of houses, duplexes and apartment buildings—later. The once-young man has become a wealthy older man who is worth millions of dollars but feels a gnawing deep inside himself that money alone will never cure. Sometimes at three or four in the morning he wakes up and realizes he has been dreaming about being a missionary. He still wants to go overseas and serve God someday, but says he can't right now. His business demands too much of his time. Friend, this man's work demands more than that; it demands his very soul!

Business is a worthy profession, and money is not inherently evil. But if God has called you to some other form of service, and you neglect the call to pursue wealth and riches, there won't be enough money in the world to cure your pain.

Earlier in this chapter, I quoted from 2 Timothy chapter 4 and Paul's description of the preacher's responsibility. It's a powerful passage, but a few verses farther down is one of the saddest sentences in the entire Bible:

> Do your best to come to me quickly, for Demas, because he loved this world, has deserted me and has gone to Thessalonica (verses 9,10).

Demas had been Paul's partner. The two of them had labored together, doing what God had called them to do. But after a time, Demas was distracted by the love of the world and left Paul to serve God alone.

I'm sure there are other ways people have devised to run from God. But no one will ever invent a foolproof method, because it's foolish to try to run from our Maker.

FINDING REAL REFUGE

In addition to all the hurricanes we experience here in the South, there's one other thing we have plenty of, and that's sand. Unfortunately, there's not much you can do with sand. It's great for walking on when the sun is setting. And it's perfect for building sand castles. But by itself it doesn't make very good building material.

Jesus' Sermon on the Mount is a wonderful collection of the Master's teaching, and at the end of the sermon, He gave this advice:

> "Therefore everyone who hears these words of mine and puts them into practice is like a wise man who built his house on the rock. The rain came down, the streams rose, and the winds blew and beat against that house; yet it did not fall, because it had its foundation on the rock.
>
> But everyone who hears these words of mine and does not put them into practice is like a foolish man who built his house on sand. The rain came down, the streams rose, and the winds blew and beat against that house, and it fell with a great crash" (Matthew 7:24-27).

What foundation are you building your life on, friend? Are you anchored on the unchanging laws of God, or are you moving this way and that on the shifting sands?

Back in the courtroom, morality and goodness are on the witness stand. Truth hangs in the balance. The closing statements have been made. It's time for the verdict. The presiding Judge raises His gavel and pronounces judgment. "The Word of God stands alone, the Holy Bible is beyond dispute. The standards of God are to be obeyed or the consequences paid." Slam! Case closed.

Notes

1. George Barna, *What Americans Believe* (Ventura, Calif.: Regal Books, 1991), pp. 83-85.
2. *Good News*, (March/April 1999), p. 42.
3. *The Watchman Expositor, 1997-1998 Index of Cults and Religions*, Vol. 14, no. 3, pp. 13, 22, 23.
4. Mark Schone, "An Awesome God," *SPIN* (Sept. 1997), pp. 112-120, 171ff.
5. Jerry Schwartz, "New Orleans Braces for Georges," Associated Press, 1998.

8

SO FAR FROM HOME

Have you ever been lost and far away from home?
I was so far gone that I thought
I would never make it back.
But I did, and I know you can, too.

Some people dismiss me when I say that no matter how far away from God you are, God can still bring you back home. They say, "That may be true for some people, preacher, but you don't know what bad shape I'm in."

Everyone is different, that's true. And I certainly don't know everyone's story. But I do know this: My preaching to people about following God isn't something I picked up in a book or seminary class. It's not just a job for me. I talk about God because God changed my life from night to day.

For me, Jesus' story of the prodigal son is more than a passage in the Bible; it's part of my life. You know that line in the song, "Amazing Grace," that goes, "I once was blind, but now I see"? That line could have been written about me. The close calls and strange occurrences I've been through could fill a year's worth of scripts for a prime-time action drama.

My purpose for writing this book is the same purpose for preaching at the Brownsville revival and at other meetings around America and the world. I do all these things for a very simple reason. I was on my way to hell. God rescued me. Now I'm on my way to heaven, and I'm taking everybody with me that I can.

In the following pages I want to share part of my story with you. I'm not bragging about the bad things I have done. In fact, I know I'm nobody special, which is something you'll be able to see pretty clearly. But over the years God has used my experiences to encourage others. Perhaps they will do that for you.

LOST WITHOUT A MAP

Some people talk about how life is a journey. If that's the case, most of the first part of my life was one long ride to nowhere. Although I was raised in a loving family, and even though my mom took me to church from the time I was a baby, my life began to veer off course.

I've told you how my dad introduced me to drinking when I was 8 years old. By the time I was 13, I was smoking pot and popping pills, while on the side I was shoplifting and stealing people's wallets and purses. By 16, I was smoking, popping, injecting and selling all kinds of drugs. I was even in a rock band. Our theme song could have been "(I Can't Get No) Satisfaction" by the Rolling Stones. I was always looking for stronger experiences, bigger risks and longer journeys away from the safety and security of my family and God's love.

That craving for more often led me out onto the road where my only constant companions were my thumb, my backpack and a deadly mixture of daring and despair.

Here are a few snapshots from my journey to hell and back.

Snapshot #1: Outside El Paso, Texas
It is hot. The air is dusty. The wind is dry. My throat is parched. I am alone and lonely. I am standing along the side of Interstate 10

with my thumb in the air. I am hitchhiking back from California. The Golden State didn't hold anything for me, so I'm heading back to sweet home Alabama.

Cars are whizzing by me at what seems like 200 miles an hour, but I'm standing as still as a cactus, and have been for what seems like hours. In fact, it seems like I've been stuck in West Texas for months.

About the only proof I have that anyone can see me is that periodically someone shouts at me while they're passing by. I can't always hear what they're shouting, but it's usually not nice words. Sometimes the words are accompanied by obscene hand gestures. Other times, drivers honk at me. And every once in a while they steer their speeding cars toward me as if they want to run me over. Or instead, they hurl a beer bottle that whizzes by my head at a velocity that would have killed me if it had hit its intended target.

Finally, someone stops. I pick up my heavy backpack and start running toward the car, which is about a hundred feet ahead of me. My head is aching, my heart is pounding and I feel like I'm about to pass out, but I know that if I run a few more feet I will be speeding down the highway toward my destination and sitting in air-conditioned comfort. Then, when I'm about six inches away from grabbing the car door, the driver speeds away. Before he disappears, he rolls down his window and shouts, "Get a job, scum!"

In between dodging more trash that people throw my way, I think about going home, sleeping in a soft bed and being somewhere where someone cares for me. I'm almost ready to cross the road and start hitching back to California when a drunk guy in a pickup truck stops and offers me a ride.

Snapshot #2: Outside Albuquerque

When hitchhikers aren't competing with each other for rides, they're sharing information about opportunities that lie ahead on the open road. Among the hot tips we always shared were the locations of rescue missions where we could find a meal or a bed, and

Red Cross shelters where we could give some blood or plasma and pick up a few bucks.

A guy I met while crossing New Mexico told me about an unemployment office outside of Albuquerque where they were hiring part-time workers for a carnival. When I got to the office, I asked how much the carnival was paying, and a man sitting on the sidewalk said, "Sixty-five cents an hour, plus shakes." Shakes are

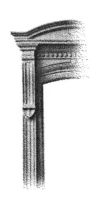

THE HARDENED HEART IS UNKNOWING AND UNBROKEN. IT IS CLOSED TO SPIRITUAL TRUTH. THE AWAKENED HEART KNOWS SOMETHING OF GOD AND WANTS TO KNOW MORE. THE BELIEVING HEART KNOWS GOD DEEPLY AND FOLLOWS HIS COMMANDS.

the carnival worker's equivalent of a waitress's tips. Only people don't give you shakes. It's what falls out of their pockets while they're on the rides. As I soon learned, an experienced ride operator can make the cars jerk in such a way to cause loose change, wallets and even purses to pile up underneath the ride.

My first day at work, I noticed a big dent in the railings of one of the rides. I asked someone what caused it. "That's where a guy landed after he did a swan dive off the top of the Ferris wheel," he told me. Life seemed unbelievably dirty and cheap.

I worked drunk most days. Once that almost caused a major accident; I failed to properly install the drive chain on the Bullet ride one day, and the whole thing went haywire when the chain suddenly broke. Fortunately, no one was hurt.

In the evenings we would all do drugs, and then I would stumble toward my little tent for the night. Some nights, before I floated off into a drug-drenched sleep, I would think about the mess I had made of my life. Here I was, the son of a middle-class family, stealing people's money and working as a greasy carny in the middle of nowhere. I didn't think life could get any lower than this.

Hints of Something Better
There are three conditions of the human heart. First there is hardness. The hardened heart is unyielding and unbroken. It is closed to spiritual truth. It wants its own way. This was the condition of my own heart during much of my life, and it is the condition many people are living in today.

But every once in a while, the dreary tedium of my life would be interrupted by a momentary glimpse of something better. Often this came through people I shared a ride or a bottle with.

The awakened heart knows something of God and wants to know more. The awakened heart is characterized by conviction. To be convicted means to be found guilty. Conviction is a good thing if you act on it. The problem was, I never did. Most of the time, any hope I experienced was quickly replaced by depression.

Finally, the believing heart knows God deeply and follows His commands. In my journeys, I met some believing people, too, but I wasn't sure they could rescue me out of my miserable condition.

Snapshot #3: In the Arizona Desert
I was hitchhiking across the desert with a newfound "friend" named Ed. When two young men in a pickup truck stopped to give us a ride, they let Ed get in the cab with the driver while the other man sat in the back of the truck with me.

We were flying through the desert, looking for the magical peyote cactus. I had photocopied a map from an old book I found in the library at the University of Arizona in Flagstaff. Some men on the Navajo Indian Reservation looked at our map and pointed out places where the cacti grew. They encouraged us to go on our search, and we knew if we found the fabled peyote, we could eat its potent "buttons," which are like a psychedelic drug but with fewer side effects.

As we sped down the highway at 60 or 70 miles an hour, I was sitting on one wheel well in the back of the truck; the other man was sitting on the wheel well across from me. We were both holding on for dear life. And then he got up from where he was sitting and slid over next to me. His action seemed dangerous, since the truck was moving so fast.

Suddenly there was a horrible explosion, and the truck sounded like it was being blown apart. We both watched in shock as a steel rod shot through the wheel well, where he had been sitting just seconds ago, and headed 100 feet straight into the air, landing on the highway behind us with a dull clang. The guy driving the truck hadn't even seen it. But if the guy in the back hadn't moved when he did, he would have been impaled by the flying metal. The shaft of steel would have ripped through his body and killed him instantly. After stopping the truck, the driver and his fortunate companion mumbled something to one another, and then we sped off down the road again.

Within a few minutes, we could see the silhouette of a church in the distance. The driver took the nearest exit, and soon we pulled into the parking lot of a small Baptist church. The driver hopped out of the truck along with his recently rescued friend, and the two ran to the church and started banging on the door. The pastor heard the banging, came out of his house near the church and greeted the two men, who pointed at us as they talked to the pastor.

The two young men walked toward us. They told us, "We don't want anything to do with you guys anymore. We've been running from God, and this was a sign from Him." They hopped into their truck and sped away, leaving us standing in front of the church with the Baptist pastor. We never saw them again. Eager to get away from that holy ground, Ed and I hiked back to the interstate, put out our thumbs and continued on our journey.

Snapshot #4: Outside Dallas

I'm hitchhiking to nowhere in particular with a longtime friend from Alabama, when we hear about an outdoor rock music festival in Dallas. Having nothing better to do, that's where we go, and by the time we get there, the concert is in full swing.

Thousands of people are listening to or dancing to the loud, rhythmic music. At some distance from the stage, we can see a brightly painted bus where people are handing out sandwiches. We grab our sandwiches and head back to the concert.

About that time the lead guitarist stops playing, puts down his instrument and begins to tell the crowd about his life. He tells us about his travels around the world with a famous rock band, his drug abuse, the parties, the sex and the whole rock-and-roll scene. Then he tells us how he got tired of the whole thing and how a friend introduced him to Jesus. I'm starting to get angry, but my friend is really listening. When the man asks if anyone in the audience would like to accept Christ, my friend immediately stands up and says, "Yes! I want to be a Christian." But I hold back.

"Listen," I tell my friend, "if you become a Christian, you'll have to cut your hair. You'll have to quit listening to rock music. And you'll have to quit drinking and doing drugs."

The reality of the decision he was facing was beginning to sink in.

"C'mon," I said, grabbing him by the arm. "Let's go get high." And we did.

ONE ROAD ENDS, ANOTHER BEGINS

I won't bore you with all the details of those horrible years. My life was a blur of drinking, drugs and criminal activity. I was jailed more than a dozen times for everything from petty crimes to sales of drugs. I would always hold odd jobs during my travels to keep money in my pocket for drugs. I even held a job for a while at a tractor factory, but for me, work was never much more than a cover for my drug abuse.

After many of my journeys, I would often return home in a desperate attempt to rest and regain my missing sanity. Home was where I found myself in the fall of 1975. I had been struggling with my growing addictions and was now suffering from violent convulsions. It was as if the Angel of Death was coming to take my life from me.

At 11:00 A.M. on October 28, I heard a knock on my bedroom door. I knew I needed help, but in my condition, I didn't want to see anyone. A man came into my room. He was the vicar of the Lutheran church where I had gone as a boy. (I later learned that my mom had called him in desperation.) He came to my bedside and began to talk to me. He said, "I know that you didn't want anything to do with me before, Steve. But I've come because you are hurting. I can't help you, but I know somebody who can. His name is Jesus, and He's here with us. He's my best friend, Steve, and He wants to help you."

I don't know why this day was so different than all the others, but I began calling out to God for help. With tears streaming down my face, I cried out, "Jesus! Jesus! Jesus! Jesus!" We were both calling out to God when something powerful took place.

Before I knew what was happening, a peace and warmth I had never known before filled my body. The convulsions that had been racking my body for days ebbed away. The walls of my room stopped pulsating and spinning. And instead of the despair that had been my constant companion for years, I began to feel the loving presence of God pervading my room and invading my heart. My journey back to God had begun. The door of heaven opened to me that day.

If you and I were watching a cheesy religious movie about my life, the action would cut away from my bed to me standing behind a pulpit at the Brownsville Assembly of God, preaching to thousands of people. But life is rarely like the movies, and shortly after accepting Christ, I found myself back in jail, the result of an outstanding warrant for my arrest on a drug charge.

The next few months were incredibly tough, but exciting. Little did I know that God was guiding my life, and that my being put in jail was all part of His master plan. It was through this experience that I was probated into a Christian drug rehabilitation program as an alternative to prison time. Soon, my life began to take on new meaning. Within a couple of years, I met my dear wife, Jeri. We married in 1979.

My new life in Christ was like a wonderful adventure. God had forgiven me, cleansed me, empowered me and given me a brand-new direction in life. He took me off the old road to nowhere that I had traveled for so many years and placed my feet on a new and exciting path.

This is why I preach with so much passion and why I'm writing this book you're reading right now. God has done amazing things for me. I know He lives, and that He saves those who turn to Him. No matter who you are, what you've done or where you've been, God is reaching out to you right now, just as He reached out to me for so many years. I was lost, but God brought me home, and He can do the same for you.

A PEOPLE GONE ASTRAY?

I love old books. The shelves of my study are full of wonderful centuries-old volumes like collections of the sermons of Jonathan Edwards, who was involved in one of America's two Great Awakenings, or Foxe's *Book of Martyrs*, covering the stories of hundreds of those who gave their lives for Christ. I have the huge leather-bound, three-volume set printed in 1694, not the short, one-volume edition available today.

One book I look at regularly is Noah Webster's *American Dictionary of the English Language*, which was published in 1849. When I'm working on a sermon, I love looking up words in this old dictionary.

As I was thinking about the journey my life has taken, I looked up the word *walk*. Look at some of the biblical definitions Webster used:

To walk with God; to live in obedience to His commands, and to have communion with Him.

To walk in darkness; to live in ignorance, error, and sin, without comfort.

To walk in the light; to live in the practice of religion, and to enjoy its consolations.

To walk by faith; to live in the firm belief of the gospel and its promises, and to rely on Christ for salvation.

To walk after the flesh; to indulge sexual appetites, and to live in sin.

To walk after the Spirit; to be guided by the counsel and influence of the Spirit and by the Word of God, and to live a life of holy deportment.

Or look at this portion of Noah Webster's definition of the word *moral:*

The word *moral* is applicable to actions that are good or evil, virtuous or vicious, and has reference to the law of God as the standard by which their character is to be determined.

You won't find biblical definitions like these in contemporary dictionaries. Why is that?

I think we all know that a person can go astray and become lost, but what about a country? Can a nation turn its back on God and go astray? Let's consider that frightening possibility for a moment.

Faith of Our Fathers

Today, many people are debating the question of whether or not America ever was a "Christian nation." It's a fascinating topic and also a complex one.

I believe that God saves individuals, not countries. Jesus died on the Cross to save you and me, not to save America or Mexico or any other country. Still, I don't think anyone doubts that some of

America's most important early leaders were sincere and devout men of faith, and that their Christian convictions shaped their political behavior and had a powerful impact on the moral direction of our country.

Just read the following comments and confessions of faith from some of our forefathers:

> I have a tender reliance on the mercy of the Almighty through the merits of the Lord Jesus Christ. I am a sinner. I look to Him for mercy.
> (Alexander Hamilton, one of America's founding fathers)

> Cursed be all that learning that is contrary to the cross of Christ.
> (James Madison, chief architect of the U.S. Constitution)

> I am a firm believer in the divine teachings, perfect example, and atoning sacrifice of Jesus Christ.
> (Rutherford B. Hayes, nineteenth president of the United States)

> I can only say that I am a poor sinner trusting in Christ alone for salvation.
> (General Robert E. Lee)

> The atonement of Jesus Christ is the only remedy and rest for my soul.
> (Martin Van Buren, eighth president of the United States)

I like new books, too, and one of the more interesting books I've seen recently is called *Material World*. This fascinating volume takes readers on a lavishly illustrated tour of people throughout the world, focusing on the possessions they have and the values they hold dear. Read the following passage by the book's primary author, Charles C. Mann:

The strains between religious belief and secular ideals have always marked U.S. history, but they have rarely been more evident than now. Although most citizens enjoy the media-saturated prosperity of the middle class, they are increasingly alarmed by the signs of what might be called "moral decay": crime, drug abuse, urban disintegration, high rates of divorce, abortion, and teenage pregnancy.[1]

Many people today are concerned about our country's moral decay. For some, this concern has led them to become more involved in politics on the local or national level. Others seem to be paralyzed by the chaos of contemporary culture, and these people seem to be able to do little more than long for the "good old days" while they grow more and more bitter and angry about the present.

Certainly, the challenge of restoring morality and decency in our country will require hard work and dedication from all of us. But in order for America to be truly on the right road, its citizens need to be on the right road themselves.

Just as God led me back to Himself after years of wandering in the darkness, perhaps He can help our country find its way back home, too. But that will happen only when we dedicate ourselves to Him, saturate our country in prayer and serve those around us with acts of love, courage and compassion. The problem with America is not "out there," it is within each and every one of us.

Note
1. Charles C. Mann et al., *Material World* (Sierra Club Books, 1994), p. 141.

Part

II

HEAVEN OPENED

God has opened His heaven on my life and ministry.
This is the way things are supposed to be.
What can we do to make intimacy with God
the pattern of our lives?

THE CREATOR
STILL CALLS

God has called you from the beginning of time.
Even now that you know Him,
He is still calling you to go deeper.

Boxer Mike Tyson had an exciting year in 1999. In January, the man who was once the world's most feared heavyweight fighter returned to the ring after serving a one-year suspension from the sport. His return to the ring resulted in a decisive victory over Francois Botha.

But then in February, Tyson's troubles returned. He was sentenced to one year in prison for assaulting motorists who had been involved in a minor auto accident with him the previous summer.

Always philosophical, Tyson explored theology with a reporter from *USA Today*:

> We all want to believe in God because we don't want to be savages—and it's politically correct to believe in God. Just in case it's true, we pray. Imagine if there is a heaven and we do have to be judged. Then we got to burn in hell.[1]

I'm sure many people turn to God to avoid the eternal punishment of hell. Sometimes, people refer to such conversions as "fire insurance." But God wants us to love Him, and fear seldom leads to love unless it's a legitimate, fearful respect for God.

God wants us to know Him. He wants us to love Him. He also wants us to let Him work in and through our lives. This deeper call of God is what we'll be talking about in this chapter.

THE TWO CALLS OF GOD

In the last seven chapters of the New Testament book of Acts, Paul tells the fascinating story of his conversion to Christianity and his later work as an evangelist. And what a dramatic conversion it was.

Paul was born and raised a Jew. In fact, his birth name was Saul, the same name given to the first king of Israel. Saul was educated at the best schools and, as he tells it, "was just as zealous for God" as those fanatical first-century Christians would one day become.

Like many Jews, Saul initially believed that Jesus was a heretic who was hell-bent on destroying Judaism, and that is why Saul became one of the Early Church's harshest persecutors. He was a one-man anti-Christian vigilante squad, or as he tells it:

> I persecuted the followers of this Way to their death, arresting both men and women and throwing them into prison, as also the high priest and all the Council can testify. I even obtained letters from them to their brothers in Damascus, and went there to bring these people as prisoners to Jerusalem to be punished (Acts 22:4,5).

A funny thing happened on the way to Damascus. A bright light from heaven flashed around Saul, causing him to fall to the ground. Then a voice cried out to him: "Saul! Saul! Why do you persecute me?"

"Who are you, Lord?" Saul asked.

"I am Jesus of Nazareth, whom you are persecuting."

"What shall I do, Lord?" Saul asked.

This was the first call of God: the outer call to acknowledge and honor God above all else. Saul responded to this call immediately and was baptized soon after. But this was just the beginning of his relationship with God.

The next important step was for Saul, who was now renamed Paul, to move from conversion to adoration, from an outward profession of Christ to an inward possession of Christ through the work of the Holy Spirit. This step involved studying the Scriptures and learning from established Christian teachers, but it also meant praying to God and allowing His Spirit to cleanse him.

Paul had many years' worth of hatred for Christ and Christians that needed to be washed away by the power of the Holy Spirit. Saul, who had persecuted the Church, was being internally transformed into Paul, who would serve the Church. A man who had spent his adult life harassing believers was about to become the victim of persecution, and over the next several years, Paul would endure imprisonment, punishment and more than one close brush with death as he traveled around the known world and preached the gospel of Jesus. Clearly, he needed more than a change of mind or profession; Paul needed a change of heart. And the Holy Spirit worked within him to create that change of heart.

I believe there are many people in churches today who have responded to the first call of God. They have acknowledged God and have asked Him to come into their lives, but it was a surface thing, at best, and didn't go much deeper.

The problem is, each individual must respond to the second call of God. He must let the Holy Spirit invade every area of his mind, heart and soul. He must ask Jesus to live within him and make him a new creation. He might know truths about God, but now he must know God in a personal and intimate way. If not, his spiritual transformation will remain superficial and incomplete.

It is my prayer that everyone reading this book will hear and accept this second call of God. Only then can we truly know God's will for our lives, as well as His daily guidance and direction.

OUR AMAZING ABILITIES

I do a fair amount of reading, but I don't get to read nearly as much as I would like. So people I work with, and other folks I know around the country, read interesting articles, make copies and send them to me. It's like having a full-time staff of researchers, and I'm always amazed by the things they find.

But consistently, one of the things I find most interesting is the never-ending process of discovery, invention and innovation that human beings all over the world are constantly involved in.

The pace of technology is moving so quickly that it's risky for me to even mention some recent inventions here. By the time this book is out, these products may have already been replaced by even more technologically advanced devices. But it's worth the risk. So here, in no particular order whatsoever, is my short list of some of the things I've read about that make me even more intrigued about humanity's amazing abilities.

Laser pointers. I know some of you may be thinking, *Been there, done that* about these little laser lights you can use to point at projection screens. But I think they're amazing. The first lasers weren't even built until the 1960s, and now anybody can get one of these for a few bucks.

Mini-memo recorders. They aren't tape recorders. We've gone way beyond that. These are about the size of a credit card, but hold a computer chip that allows you to record your voice. They cost $10 to $20, and most people use them to keep track of ideas, memos, shopping lists and things like that. I keep one handy in my car for recording sermon thoughts that come to me while I'm driving.

Bullet trains. OK, these cost more than a few bucks. Try a few hundred million. But they have them in Japan and Europe, and they whisk people down the tracks at 160 miles per hour or more.

Fiber-optic cables. Phone lines used to be big fat monstrosities, but now a tiny fiber-optic cable can transmit thousands of phone calls simultaneously. Hey, maybe I'm easily amazed, but you're talking to a guy who is still pretty impressed by telephones. Just about every day our office receives calls from Argentina or Russia or Japan, and the callers sound like they're in the house down the road, not on the other side of the world.

Face recognition security. I know, this sounds like something right out of a James Bond movie, but companies are working on security devices that "read" the face—or sometimes the eyes—of visitors so you can tell whether the person at your front door is a friend or foe. Somebody is going to walk up to your house and your house is going to recognize who it is. Friend, the brawny builders of the Tower of Babel would have been blown away by the mention of such awesome technological wonders.

Automatic debit cards. This technology might be voice recognition-activated, or it may use a computer chip. But either way, when you go shopping, you won't have to lug around a wallet or purse full of cash and credit cards; the store will be able to access your account information and deduct the amount needed to cover your purchases. Some people say we're heading for a cash-free society. I don't know when that will happen, but the technology is just around the corner.

Nanotechnology. This is the ability to shrink the size of equipment to the point where machines are approaching the size of molecules. For example, in the medical field, they now have microscopic cameras that can be mounted to the end of a tiny threadlike tube that can travel through your body taking movies of your guts. May not sound like a great film to you, but to doctors trying to detect heart problems or kidney stones, these tiny cameras are great technology.

Space exploration. From tiny cameras in our own "inner space" to massive spaceships like the Voyager probe, cameras can now travel 390 million miles to Jupiter and take pictures, capturing

Kodak moments of outer space and sending them back for us to look at, making us the first human beings to ever see these fascinating scenes that God has been looking at for eons.

I could go on and on, listing these kinds of things. Perhaps I'm easily entertained, but don't you think it's fantastic some of the capabilities God has given humanity and what we have done with those abilities?

The Most Powerful Ability of All
Impressive as all of these inventions and developments are, there is another remarkable ability I would like you to think about. This capability that you and I have is also God-given, but it has caused more damage to our world than all the wars in all of human history combined. It has brought more destruction of families, more suicides and more divorces than any of us could possibly fathom. This one thing has changed the course of history millions and millions of times, and it has often brought eternally devastating results.

This ability I would like you to think about is the ability we have to resist the Holy Spirit. God didn't make us all robots. He didn't program us to love Him, because programmed love wouldn't really be love at all. But the danger of this freedom we have been given is that when we resist the Holy Spirit—as millions of people are doing today—we are turning our backs on the second call of God.

Let's think about this for a moment by comparing it to the medical profession. Imagine God as an emergency room doctor who saves our lives. We have been tempting fate and dancing with danger until we find ourselves in a really tight spot—like I was with my growing addiction problem. So we pray for God to save us, and God does.

After we get out of the emergency room and are transported to the recovery wing of the hospital, another doctor decides he wants to sit down and have a long chat with us about our lifestyles, our bad decisions and all our destructive habits that keep placing us in danger and bringing us back to the emergency room for repair.

This other doctor can be compared to the Holy Spirit. We've

already been saved, and we aren't in danger of dying. But the Spirit knows that unless we change our lifestyles, our salvation will be short-lived or superficial. Serious change is needed. We need to change our diets; we need to cut out some of the evil things we used to consume so they don't poison our lives anymore. We need to change our behav-

BEING SAVED ISN'T THE END OF THE CHRISTIAN LIFE, IT'S JUST THE BEGINNING. WE HAVE YEARS AND YEARS OF ACCUMULATED JUNK TO GET OUT OF OUR SYSTEMS. AND THAT'S WHERE THE HOLY SPIRIT COMES IN.

ior so we don't find ourselves in compromising situations any longer. The Holy Spirit probes us about these deeper inner changes that are required to make our salvation continue and grow.

We all have the ability to resist the Holy Spirit, but does that really make any sense? That's like going to a doctor with a broken leg but refusing to allow him to inspect the leg or put it in a cast. Instead of allowing the seasoned medical professional to heal us and put us back on the road to recovery, we hide under the covers and scream out, "Don't touch me, that hurts!"

Healing just about always hurts, my friend. When you get a flu shot, the needle stings for a moment. There's no denying that. But unless that needle injects the healing medicine into your blood-stream, the winter flu bug is likely to get you. And when it does, it will multiply and multiply, making you sicker and sicker. Then you have to take medicine to get the infection out of your body. It's the same way with God. Being saved isn't the end of the Christian life, it's just the beginning. After being saved, we have years and years of accumulated junk to get out of our systems. And that's where the Holy Spirit comes in.

When we hide from doctors, we treat them like the enemy instead of letting them use their training and knowledge to help us get better. Sadly, some of us treat God the same way. He has saved us, but we don't want to let Him cleanse and renew us. We hear the first call of God, but we remain deaf or disobedient to the second call. Remember, God doesn't want to hurt us; He wants to heal us.

The Spirit Convicts
Just like getting a flu shot, the Holy Spirit's work can hurt, at least initially.

In Acts chapter 2, Peter is empowered by the Holy Spirit and preaches a powerful sermon about Jesus. He invites everyone within the sound of his voice to accept Jesus, before concluding with this sentence:

> Therefore let all Israel be assured of this: God has made this Jesus, whom you crucified, both Lord and Christ (Acts 2:36).

The next verse describes his audience's reaction:

> When the people heard this, they were cut to the heart and said to Peter and the other apostles, "Brothers, what shall we do?"

Their response was similar to Paul's when he was confronted by the truth about Jesus. Even though the message was shocking, even painful, and they were "cut to the heart," they moved beyond the pain to acceptance and healing.

The Holy Spirit is in the business of convicting us of our sin and our need for God's righteousness. As Paul told the Thessalonians,

"Our gospel came to you not simply with words, but also with power, with the Holy Spirit and with deep conviction" (1 Thessalonians 1:5). In his epistle, Jude tells us that "the Lord is coming with thousands upon thousands of his holy ones to judge everyone, and to convict all the ungodly of all the ungodly acts they have done in the ungodly way" (Jude 14,15).

The Gospel of John speaks of the Holy Spirit more than any other Gospel. John tells us about the coming of the Spirit (or as John called Him, the "Counselor"). Listen to these words of Jesus as He tells His disciples about the coming of the Spirit:

> "But I tell you the truth: It is for your good that I am going away. Unless I go away, the Counselor will not come to you; but if I go, I will send him to you. When he comes, he will convict the world of guilt in regard to sin and righteousness and judgment....When he, the Spirit of truth, comes, he will guide you into all truth" (John 16:7,8,13).

Conviction hurts, at least at first. But after the pain comes healing and joy, for the Spirit wants to bring the fullness of God into our lives.

The Spirit Empowers

The book of Acts describes how the Holy Spirit empowered the Early Church to spread the Word and do amazing miracles. One of the believers who was most powerfully empowered by God was Stephen, a person Acts describes as "a man full of faith and of the Holy Spirit."

Acts also tells us that "Stephen, a man full of God's grace and power, did great wonders and miraculous signs among the people. Opposition arose, however, from members of the Synagogue" (Acts 6:8,9). Some of Stephen's opponents sought to silence him, but they themselves were silenced instead because "they could not stand up against his wisdom or the Spirit by whom he spoke" (verse 10).

So Stephen's opponents did the next best thing: They hauled him before the Sanhedrin—the religious ruling council—using the false charges that Stephen had blasphemed God. This set the stage for Stephen to deliver one of the longest sermons found in the New Testament, which is 52 verses long and spreads over several pages of the Bible. I'm talking here about the inward call of God.

All the members of the Sanhedrin looked at Stephen, whose "face was like the face of an angel," as the high priest asked him, "Are these charges true?" (Acts 7:1).

Beginning with the plea, "Brothers and fathers, listen to me" (verse 2), Stephen launched into a sermon that covered all the high points of Jewish history, including the lives of Abraham, Isaac, Jacob, Joseph, Moses, Aaron, David and Solomon, before closing with this aggressive challenge:

> You stiff-necked people, with uncircumcised hearts and ears! You are just like your fathers: You always resist the Holy Spirit! (Acts 7:51).

Stephen's message convicted the Sanhedrin's members about their hard hearts, but instead of allowing the Spirit's conviction to bring conversion, they turned on Stephen, dragging him out of the city and stoning him to death. As he was dying, Stephen voiced two prayers to God: "Lord Jesus, receive my spirit" and "Lord, do not hold this sin against them" (Acts 7:59,60).

It wasn't Stephen's skill as a public speaker that enabled him to communicate in such a powerful way; it was the empowering of the Holy Spirit. It wasn't Stephen's courage and bravery that enabled him to stand before his accusers in the Sanhedrin and proclaim the gospel; it was the empowering of the Holy Spirit. It wasn't Stephen's personal strength that enabled him to be faithful to Christ as the stones his accusers hurled at him struck him down and killed him; it was the empowering of the Holy Spirit.

The very same Spirit who empowered Stephen nearly 2,000

years ago empowers men and women around the world today. This is God's second call. Will you answer it and accept God's blessings and power?

The Spirit at Work

By the time this book comes out in the summer of 1999, the revival in Brownsville will have been going on for more than four years. More than three million people will have come to the revival, and hundreds of thousands will have come down to the altar to get right with God.

This shouldn't come as any great surprise to you, but the people like myself, John Kilpatrick, Lindell Cooley, Michael Brown and others who have been involved in the revival are not the smartest and most articulate people in the world. This revival isn't continuing because of our superior skills or abilities. Instead, this revival continues to change lives night after night because the Spirit is working here in power.

Not everybody sees things that way. We have many critics. Some have called Brownsville a "counterfeit revival." Some have called me a false prophet.

Jesus said you will know them by their fruit. How can this be anything less than genuine when hundreds of thousands of lives have been totally changed by the power of God? I'll be sharing a few of these stories in the next chapter.

Revivals have always had critics. The First Great Awakening, which was a series of revivals that transformed the American colonies between 1725 and 1760, had many outspoken critics. Charles Finney, who preached in the 1800s and is now heralded as the father of modern revivalism, was criticized in his day. The Azusa Street revival of the early twentieth century had many critics. G. Campbell Morgan, an evangelist from England, called Azusa Street "the last vomit of Satan." H. A. Ironside called the behavior at this modern Pentecostal outpouring "disgusting, delusions, insanities, exhibitions worthy of a madhouse."[2]

Brownsville has experienced its share of criticism, but I'm too busy ministering to people to stop and debate the critics. Thousands of people are meeting Jesus for the first time, and thousands more are getting to know Him better and are experiencing healing, renewing and refreshing from God. For us, continuing this great work is more important than arguments and hair-splitting.

The great German evangelist Reinhard Bonnke was asked why he didn't take time to answer his critics. His reply was classic: "I'm on a combine in the harvest fields of the Lord. I'm not going to get off to chase a mouse."

God's Invader

The Holy Spirit is at work all over the world today. In India, entire villages are converting to Christ, even though these new believers face intense persecution. In England, evangelism programs like Alpha are bringing a fresh aroma of Christ to a country that is steeped in centuries of dead religion. Throughout Africa, Christianity is growing at a faster pace than Islam, even though many African governments lend their support to Muslims and harass or kill Christians. And in China, a country where opposition to Christianity is intense and entrenched, revival is flowering and the Church is growing, largely through the ministry of thousands of small but intense house churches that, to many people, seem remarkably similar to the first Christian churches we read about in the book of Acts.

The Holy Spirit is working everywhere that people allow Him to work, for as one British pastor put it,

The Holy Ghost is an invader. He does not belong to this natural sphere. He is a supernatural being. He comes from over the border. His origin is the great beyond. He breaks into the area of everyday existence from without. Despite all the restraints that men may erect to keep him out, he mows down every barrier and will have right of way. But although he is other than ourselves, the Holy Spirit is not hostile, save to sin. He has no malign intent towards our persons. He does not come to destroy anything but evil. He is a benevolent invasion. He comes to bring a blessing.[3]

Won't you let the Spirit invade your life and your heart? Say yes to the second call of God.

Notes

1. Mike Tyson, USA Today (January 12, 1999), Section C.
2. Vinson Synan, The Holiness Pentecostal Movement in the United States, reprint (Grand Rapids: William B. Eerdmans Publishing Co., 1983), p. 144.
3. A. Skevington Wood, Baptised with Fire (Glasgow: Pickering & Inglis Ltd., 1958), p. 127.

THE LONG ROAD HOME

Nothing is over until God says it is over.
And just as Jesus raised people from the dead,
the risen Jesus can raise us to new life in Him.

God speaks to us in many different ways. He frequently uses the Scriptures, which are His written revelation to humanity. He often uses preachers or wise Christian men and women who have known Him for a long time. He can also communicate to our hearts when we pray, or through the circumstances in our lives.

Sometimes, when we are particularly thickheaded and closed-hearted, God devises more creative ways to get our attention. In at least one case, God communicated to a human being through a donkey (see Numbers 22).

One method God often uses to communicate His wisdom to me is dreams, and I'll never forget one especially vivid dream God gave me early one morning.

In this dream, I was driving down the road on my way to a church. As I pulled up to the church, I noticed that a big black funeral hearse adorned with flowers was parked in front of the building. It was a sobering sight, because I had not planned on attending a funeral that day.

I parked my car and made my way past some of the mourners who had gathered around the hearse. I wanted to get a closer look at the curious scene before me.

To my amazement, the casket was not positioned lengthwise in the hearse, but was lying across the tailgate. There were people standing around, moaning and groaning with grief.

When I looked down into the open coffin, I saw a man with his arms crossed on his chest in the typical manner. His face, which was covered with makeup, looked as if it had been treated for burial. But when I looked closer at his face, I noticed his lips were moving.

Suddenly alarmed, I looked at the people and began pointing at the man. "Look!" I screamed. "Excuse me! EXCUSE ME! This man isn't dead, he's alive!"

They all looked at me with shock and disbelief. One of the men who was involved in the funeral arrangements looked sternly at me and said, "This is his funeral. He is dead."

He tried to shoo me away, but I wouldn't be silenced, and I said to the stern man, "Sir, look at his lips. They're moving. This man is trying to talk!"

The second I said these words, the man sitting behind the hearse's steering wheel started the car, slammed his foot on the accelerator until it hit the floor, and sped off down the street.

When I awoke from this surreal experience, I wondered, *What is God trying to tell me with this strange dream?*

Not Dead, Only Sleeping

There is an amazing story about death and life that appears three times in the New Testament. It concerns a man whose daughter had died and the desperate appeal he made to Jesus:

And one of the synagogue officials named Jairus came up, and upon seeing [Jesus], fell at His feet, and entreated Him earnestly, saying, "My little daughter is at the point of death; please come and lay your hands on her, that she may get well and live."

And [Jesus] went off with him; and a great multitude was following Him and pressing in on Him....

While [Jesus] was still speaking, [people] came from the house of the synagogue official, saying, "Your daughter has died; why trouble the Teacher anymore?" But Jesus, overhearing what was being spoken, said to the synagogue official, "Do not be afraid any longer, only believe."

And He allowed no one to follow with Him, except Peter and James and John the brother of James. And they came to the house of the synagogue official; and [Jesus] beheld a commotion, and people loudly weeping and wailing. And entering in, He said to them, "Why make a commotion and weep? The child has not died, but is asleep."

And they began laughing at Him. But putting them all out, He took along the child's father and mother and His own companions, and entered the room where the child was. And taking the child by the hand, He said to her, "Talitha kum!" (which translated means, "Little girl, I say to you, arise!")

And immediately the girl rose and began to walk; for she was twelve years old. And immediately they were completely astounded (Mark 5:22-24,35-42, *NASB*).

The lesson we need to learn from this is that it isn't over until Jesus says it's over. And this case isn't the only instance where Jesus raised a dead person to life. As a matter of fact, Jesus messed up every funeral He attended. Probably the best known example involved a man named Lazarus, who was the brother of Mary and Martha, two women who were followers of Jesus.

Lazarus had been sick for some time, and the two sisters sent word to Jesus, asking Him to heal their brother's illness. But Jesus wasn't able to be with Lazarus right away. By the time He arrived at the man's village, Lazarus had already died and had been buried four days. But once again, Jesus amazed an unbelieving crowd when He raised Lazarus from the dead. Before He arrived in Bethany, He had told His disciples, "Our friend Lazarus has fallen asleep; but I am going there to wake him up" (John 11:11).

Once again, it isn't over until Jesus says it's over. Just a few verses later, Jesus delivers one of the most powerful messages in the entire Bible:

> "I am the resurrection and the life. He who believes in me will live, even though he dies; and whoever lives and believes in me will never die. Do you believe this?" (John 11:25,26).

What about you, friend? Do you believe Jesus could perform amazing miracles like this while He walked on the earth? Even more importantly, do you believe that Jesus, who Himself rose from the dead and now sits at the right hand of God the Father, can give us eternal life? Do you believe this?

Not Dead Yet

I don't know if you've ever seen a dead body, but there are many telltale signs to let you know someone is physically deceased. First, the skin begins to turn a gray, ashen color. Then the nail beds turn a dusty blue—a sure indication that the body is no longer getting any life-giving oxygen.

There are also telltale signs that someone is spiritually dead, although it is sometimes difficult to tell for sure. I once showed many advanced signs of spiritual death. I was listless and depressed. I constantly tried to drown my sorrows in alcohol and mask them with drugs. Sometimes I couldn't get out of bed for days. Just about everyone but my mama—and God—had given up on me, and I'm thankful they didn't.

Let me say something right now to mothers and fathers everywhere: Don't you ever give up on your sons and daughters. Sure, there are times when things look impossible, when circumstances look so bleak that you don't think there's a snowball's chance in hell that your son or daughter is going to turn around. You may feel like giving up on them, but don't give up on God. Pray for your children. Get down on your knees and ask God to bring them home to Him. Don't get caught up in despair and negativism. Don't start believing that God can't do the very things He can do. God is a God of miracles. Jesus is still raising Lazaruses.

GOD IS A GOD OF LOST CAUSES AND LOST PEOPLE. NOTHING—ABSOLUTELY NOTHING—IS IMPOSSIBLE WITH GOD. AND NOTHING IS OVER UNTIL HE SAYS IT IS.

And let me say something to you if you believe things are bleak. Perhaps you're struggling with a temptation that has troubled you for years, or maybe you're heading into a new and uncertain period of life. Don't give up on God. The Creator of the universe can create a new life and a new heart within you. It isn't over until He says it's over.

There's a psalm written by Asaph that speaks to us all about sorrow and hope, about the fear that God is far away, and the faith that He can still save us. First, read these despairing words:

> I cried out to God for help;
>> I cried out to God to hear me.
> When I was in distress, I sought the Lord;
>> at night I stretched out untiring hands

and my soul refused to be comforted.
I remembered you, O God, and I groaned;
    I mused, and my spirit grew faint....
You kept my eyes from closing;
    I was too troubled to speak (Psalm 77:1-4).

After a time of sadness and despair, Asaph remembered how big God is. Now read his words of faith and trust:

Then I thought, "To this I will appeal:
    the years of the right hand of the Most High."
I will remember the deeds of the Lord;
    yes, I will remember your miracles of long ago."
I will meditate on all your works
    and consider all your mighty deeds (verses 10-12).

Friend, don't forget this: God is a God of lost causes and lost people. Nothing—absolutely nothing—is impossible with God. And nothing is over until He says it is.

TESTIMONIES OF THE RISEN

The Brownsville revival has been going on for more than four years now, and during that time, multiplied thousands of people who believed their lives were dead and done have come forward to the altar and given their hearts to God. I never get a chance to talk to most of these people, but hundreds of them have written long tear-stained letters to me, detailing the "death" of their lives before they knew God, and the "resurrection" that Jesus brought them when they asked Him to save them. Let me briefly share a few of those letters with you. Remember, my friend, if God can do it for these people, He can do it for you. If the door of heaven swings open for them, why wouldn't it open for you? The Bible says that God is no respecter of persons (see Acts 10:34).

Michelle, who was 28 when she wrote, said Satan had stolen her innocence when she was only four years old. That's when her grandfather—who was a professing Christian—began sexually abusing her. Later, her brother repeatedly raped her. After years of suicide attempts, sexual permissiveness and drug abuse, Michelle wound up homeless and unable to support her children. Things looked bleak, indeed.

"Then I reached out to God on September 10, 1997," she writes. She wound up at a rescue mission that helps people who are down-and-out, and later at a Brownsville revival service, where she met Jesus. "I fell so in love with Him," she wrote. "Satan has no hold on me anymore."

Ronald wrote that he "was raised up in a small country Baptist church, where I was dragged to church every time the doors were open." Baptized at age 12, Ronald began to be tempted by the world at around age 16, "and my backsliding began." Married and divorced, he began running around with married women. "In July 1995, I was so unsatisfied with my life I even contemplated suicide."

Ronald remarried, and this time his wife began taking him to church, where the couple recommitted their lives to the Lord before visiting the Brownsville revival, where Ronald was confronted with the challenge of holy living. "God showed me some things that were not right in my home," he wrote. "It hit home when you said, 'If you are going to say you are a Christian, then live like a Christian.' "

Amy wrote about how her mother had left an abusive husband and later separated from a second husband. "Every man that came into my life either abandoned me or was taken from me," she wrote. After years of sexual experimentation and alcohol abuse, Amy came to Brownsville, where she returned to the altar night after night. "God was freeing me of the bondage of my sin," she wrote. Now she is on her way to being a missionary. "I have a fire in me for God that I never thought I'd have," she writes.

It's not over until God says it's over, my friend.

If this book had a few thousand more pages, I could only begin to tell you some of the hundreds and hundreds of amazing stories people share with us about wasted and hopeless lives that have been supernaturally transformed by God.

There's the E-mail message from Eric, a pastor's son, who was molested at an early age, became gay, was kicked out of a Christian college and came back to God. There's the six-page, handwritten letter from Carmen, a woman who had been delivered from involvement in the occult, who wrote, "All my life I felt like a worthless burden because people told me I was." There was the three-page typed letter from Anna, who said, "This revival has saved my life."

Friend, this is not an ad for Brownsville. We're nothing special. But God *is* something special, and no situation is too far gone for Him to redeem it.

CONFRONTING THE CONSEQUENCES OF SIN

On October 28, 1975, after years of running from God, I ran *to* Him, asking Him to come into my life. Almost immediately, I felt the peace of His presence comforting my troubled soul. But that wasn't the end of my long road back home to where God wanted me to be.

Sins I had committed before I accepted Christ were still catching up with me. God forgives us for our sins, friend. There's no question about that. But God does not always step in to prevent us from experiencing the horrible consequences of our sin.

Men and women who have been sexually promiscuous can receive God's forgiveness and become like virgins again, but that doesn't mean they won't have to deal with problems like unplanned pregnancies or sexually transmitted diseases. A man who has spent years lying to his friends and cheating his business associates can be forgiven and renewed by God, but some of the folks he defrauded over the years might stay pretty upset at him until he works to make things right.

Shortly after I came to Christ, an old drug deal came back to haunt me, and I was sentenced to two years in jail. But after a short time, I was released to a treatment program run by a godly man named Jim Summers, who discipled me in the things of God. The time I spent with Jim was good for me. But it wasn't until my time had been served that I received release from my obligation to the state. I can still remember the day I received this document in the mail:

STATE BOARD OF PARDONS AND PAROLES
Montgomery, Alabama
CERTIFICATE GRANTING RESTORATION OF
CIVIL AND POLITICAL RIGHTS

Know All Men By These Presents:

It having been made to appear to the Alabama State Board of Pardons and Paroles that Stephen Lawrence Hill WM Cir. Ct. #75-12-870F was convicted in Madison County on February 9, 1976 of Possession and Sale of [narcotics] and was sentenced to a term of 2 years and was placed on probation for a term of 2 years; and the probation period has now been terminated by the Court, and [sic]

It further appearing to the Board from the official report of the Probation and Parole Supervisor which is a part of the record of this case, and with no further information to the contrary, that the above named has so conducted himself since release as to demonstrate his reformation and to merit restoration of civil and political rights;

NOW, in compliance with the authority vested in the

State Board of Pardons and Paroles by the constitution and the Laws of the State of Alabama to restore civil and political rights, it is:

ORDERED, that the loss of all civil and political rights resulting from the above stated conviction and any prior disqualifying convictions be and they are hereby restored.

GIVEN UNDER THE HAND AND SEAL
of the State Board of Pardons and Paroles,
the 7th day of June, 1977

STATE BOARD OF PARDONS AND PAROLES
By (Executive Director)

For me, and for most other people, coming to Jesus isn't the end of struggles and trials. It is merely the beginning of a new and very long road. But at least when you are on God's path, the struggles of life are leading you somewhere. Life is no longer a series of downward spirals, but a growth in God's grace that transforms our lives and gives us a preview of the joys of eternal life.

The Road to Repentance
Many people who turn to religion aren't thinking about God at all; they're just thinking about what's in it for them. This self-centered approach to spirituality might explain why New Age religions are so popular with so many people today. People want an easy and painless way to be connected with God.

But it's time for a reality check, here. There is no painless way to God. I agree with what pollster George Gallup Jr. said:

Spirituality is the buzzword of our time. People embrace it because it lets them feel good. They claim to seek the fruits of faith, but do so without understanding the obligations true spirituality requires. This superficial understanding ultimately leads to the glorification of self, not God. Spirituality without moral content is hollow.[1]

Christianity allows people to feel good about some things, but it doesn't do so without making us all experience a little old-fashioned guilt and remorse. It's not that God wants us to feel bad. It's just that He doesn't want us to be superficial about how serious sin is, how much it hurts us and how much it cost Jesus to die for us and take our sin away. Remember, to be a Christian is to be a follower of Christ. It means you adhere to and follow His holy teaching.

One of the things we preach about a lot at the Brownsville revival is repentance. That's a word you won't hear in many churches, but I believe it's at the root of making a right response to a holy God. I believe repentance—which means changing the direction of our lives 180 degrees and turning our backs on sin in all its forms—is a prerequisite for knowing and loving God deeply.

Peter Marshall and David B. Manuel, authors of the book *From Sea to Shining Sea*, agree:

> The key to revival has always been repentance. Before God will pour out His Spirit on all flesh, an individual and corporate turning away from sin and self, to God, must occur. No other way—no cheap grace; no putting the country ahead of God; none of the "we're God's Chosen People, and we know that He will see us through, no matter what" kind of thinking, [which] too many Christians like to comfort themselves with these days, will suffice. Repentance is the missing ingredient in much of modern American Christianity.[2]

Turning to God isn't a simple one-step process, folks. It isn't like ordering a burger at a drive-thru window or getting a soda out of a machine. It isn't a quick, neat, self-serve, one-size-fits-all transition. As the motto says, "No pain, no gain." And frequently, even though the long road to God may begin with intense joy, it takes pain, suffering and determination to walk with God all the way to the end.

Referring to the repentance message, Steve Beard, in the March/April issue of the United Methodist magazine, *Good News*, writes,

> I sit nervously throughout the entire sermon, feeling the Holy Spirit poke and prod my heart, revealing my sin and seeming to say, "Let's get this stuff out of here."
>
> Evangelist Steve Hill has been thundering from the pulpit four nights a week since Father's Day 1995. The message is the same each night with a slightly different twist: *Get the sin out of your life and get your life right with God! Hell is real,* he says, *Jesus is the way out.* It is the old-fashioned hellfire and brimstone preaching, the message of eternal truth carried by the early Methodist circuit riders. To modern ears, however, it is downright terrifying.[3]

The Road to Freedom

Knowing God brings true peace, deep relief and a powerful sense of thankfulness and joy. Repenting of sin enables us to slip free from sin's clutching grasp, allowing us to breathe free once again.

I thank God that I had the opportunity to study under Leonard Ravenhill, a powerful man of God, legendary revivalist and author of books like *Why Revival Tarries*. Leonard would often hand me a book, look me in the eye and say, "Steve, don't just go through this book, but let this book go through you."

Once when he said that to me, he was giving me a copy of a book by John Gregory Mantle. The following passage from the book shows that even though repentance must lead us through some dark times, God doesn't want us to stay in the catacombs:

> The French have a most suggestive proverb: "He is not escaped who drags his chain!"
>
> Gibbon tells of one of the Roman emperors who was

brought from prison to the palace, and who sat for some hours on the throne with his fetters on his limbs. Thousands of those whom God has brought out of prison are in much the same condition. They are in the palace, but they carry about them vestiges of the prison-life. They have escaped from the tyrant's custody, but they are not yet completely free; for as the grim jailer hears the rattle of the links sin has forged, and sees some of his fetters upon the soul, he still exercises his power, and indulges the hope that he may one day seize and entirely enslave his former captives.

So long as we fail to perceive and claim deliverance from the power of indwelling sin through the wondrous Cross, we may give occasional evidence of our kingship, but we shall give unmistakable proof of our servitude.[4]

Growth in the faith certainly requires self-examination, a process Thomas Watson describes as "setting up a court of conscience and keeping a register there, that by a strict scrutiny a man may see how matters stand between God and his soul."[5] But self-examination can only lead so far, and those who don't understand this can become totally self-absorbed.

After all, our growth in grace doesn't come from putting our lives under a microscope and staring at it hour after hour. Rather, growth in grace comes from God's supernatural work in our lives. I like how Watchman Nee, a Chinese Christian who suffered greatly for his faith, expressed this idea:

I have illustrated this from the electric light. You are in a room and it is growing dark. You would like to have the light on in order to read. There is a reading lamp on the table beside you. What do you do? Do you watch it intently to see if the light will come on? Do you take a cloth and polish the bulb? No, you get up and cross over to the other side of the room where the switch is on the wall, and you turn the current on. You turn your attention to the source of power and, when you have taken the necessary action there, the light comes on here. So in our walk with the Lord our attention must be fixed on Christ.[6]

In the long road, it's neither our spiritual "togetherness" nor our deep remorse for sin that will take us further down the road toward our destination with God. It's only a minute-by-minute dependence on His love and His grace that will complete our transformation and make us new men and women in God.

It was God's grace that initially gave us new life instead of the living death we knew before. And ultimately, it will be His grace working in us that brings us home.

Notes
1. George Gallup Jr., *Emerging Trends* 19 (June 1997), p. 1.
2. Peter Marshall and David B. Manuel, *From Sea to Shining Sea* (Grand Rapids: Baker Book House, 1985), p. 405.
3. Steve Beard, *Good News*, (March/April 1999), p. 32.
4. John Gregory Mantle, *Beyond Humiliation: The Way of the Cross* (Washington, D.C.: Testimony Books Ministry, 1974), p. 41.
5. Thomas Watson, *A Body of Practical Divinity* (Aberdeen, Scotland, George King, 1838), pp. 494, 95.
6. Watchman Nee, *The Normal Christian Life* (Wheaton, Ill.: Tyndale House Publishers, 1977), p. 84.

11

ONE OF THESE DAYS IS NONE OF THESE DAYS

God is loving and patient, and
He wants to open heaven to us.
So why postpone accepting
everything He has to offer?
God's love is forever, but the
time of salvation is now.

When I was a kid growing up in Alabama, I decided one day that I was going to be a pumpkin king. I planted hundreds of pumpkin seeds all over our backyard, watered them, and watched in amazement as the plants began to grow like weeds.

Before long I could see tiny little green pumpkin buds popping up on the stems, and after that, increasingly large, gorgeous, golden-colored gourds.

Every day I would tend to my crop, and as I walked around the yard, I would examine the pumpkins, seeing which one might turn out to be the world's largest. Although I initially intended to give them away, I now began calculating all the money I could make from selling my crop to all our neighbors. Of course, my mama would get a free pumpkin so she could bake us some of her delicious pies. Everybody else would have to pay.

When it came time to harvest my crop, I felt overwhelmed by the task that lay before me. These were big pumpkins, my friend. Some of them weighed 20 pounds or more. Picking, cleaning and hauling them was beginning to look like it would be a major operation. And the fact that they were ripening right as the summer sun was at its hottest and the air was at its most humid didn't help matters any.

I kept delaying the inevitable until one day Mama asked me when I was going to pick my pumpkins. "They'll go bad if you don't pick them," she told me. "Okay," I told her, trying to find a way to put off the chore for one more day. "I'll do it tomorrow."

That night, my deep sleep was interrupted by loud banging noises that sounded like a series of shotguns going off. I jumped out of bed and looked out my window, and the sight I saw sent shivers down my spine. The pavement outside my window was being pelted by golf ball-sized hail, and what's worse, the hail was pulverizing my pumpkins into a slimy, orange mess.

As soon as the sun came up, I went out in the yard to inspect my crop. Nearly every pumpkin had been destroyed; only a few small ones had survived. My mama tried to console me, but I would not be consoled. I was heartbroken. All the work I had put into those pumpkins had gone to waste, and all I was left with was one huge stinking, rotting mess.

I didn't realize it at the time, but my little experiment in agribusiness had given me a valuable lesson about plants, as well as life: You need to harvest things when the time is ripe, because if you wait too long, you may be too late.

To Everything a Season

In the 1960s, there was a band named the Byrds that had a number of hits from recording songs written by Bob Dylan. But in

December 1965, the Byrds had a number-one hit with a song written by somebody who was much older and wiser than Dylan. The song was called "Turn, Turn, Turn," and even though the melody was by folk musician Pete Seeger, the words were originally written by the Old Testament wise man Solomon:

> There is a time for everything, and a season for every activity under heaven: a time to be born and a time to die, a time to plant and a time to uproot (Ecclesiastes 3:1,2).

I believe Solomon may have been talking about more than pumpkins here, and as I look through the Bible, one theme I see appearing time and again is the idea that there is a set time for each one of us to respond to God's mercy.

There are two brief verses tucked away in the Bible that express this idea in subtle but powerful ways. Near the end of his second letter to Timothy, Paul includes these interesting comments: "Erastus stayed in Corinth, and I left Trophimus sick in Miletus. Do your best to get here before winter" (2 Timothy 4:20,21).

On the surface this comment seems too simple to warrant much attention, but I find it fascinating. Erastus, who has been working with Paul, stays behind and does not accompany Paul any further. We don't know the reasons why. Trophimus, another coworker, is sick. Paul, who had been able to perform so many healing miracles through the course of his ministry, was unable to heal one of his closest partners.

One can detect the emotion in his heart as Paul pleads to Timothy: "Do your best to get here before winter." Perhaps Paul feels lonely and doesn't want to head into the winter months alone. The trials and fatigue that have accompanied Paul on every step of his lengthy missionary journeys may be wearing him down physically and emotionally. He wants Timothy's sympathy and companionship, and he wants it now, not later. Have you ever felt this kind of longing for companionship and support?

Have you ever been caught alone out in a winter storm? The temperature is freezing, the wind is howling, the blowing snow stings your skin and makes it impossible to see your hands or feet. It's dangerous to be out in such conditions. If the cold temperatures don't get you, dehydration can. Weather like this doesn't hit Alabama as often as it does Minnesota, but on a symbolic level, God is trying to tell us that there's a wintertime coming for each and every one of us.

The other verse I want you to consider is from the prophet Jeremiah:

The harvest is past,

the summer has ended,

and we are not saved (Jeremiah 8:20).

As with Solomon, Jeremiah is talking about more than climate and agriculture. He is describing the challenges we all face from time to time.

Jeremiah, who was a prophet of God, was speaking during a turbulent and socially chaotic time (sound familiar?). God had given him the ability to see the destruction of Judah, which was one of the Jewish kingdoms. Judah was lost in sin, and its citizens had not taken advantage of the many opportunities God had given them to return to Him. Now, the times of opportunity—or harvest—were past, and winter was at hand. The door that God had so graciously opened was now closing. God's patience was expiring.

Some of you reading this page right now are in the summer of your life. Things couldn't be going better. You have your health. You share love with family members and fun with friends. You have a job or other activities that bring you enjoyment and use your abilities. But will these good times last? What will you do and where will you turn if you are stripped of everything you have, like the Old Testament character Job?

Winter is coming for all of us. The grass that is now soft and green will one day turn brown and brittle. The green leaves will burst into glorious color only to dry up and blow away. In some ways the animals are smarter than we are. They are storing up food for the long hard winter because they know it's going to be many months before they can eat plants and berries again.

My plea to you right now is that you make every effort to get your life right with God before the leaves fall from the trees and the petals fall from the flowers. Don't be like a lost man caught out in a blizzard. Find warmth now while it can be found. Fortify your faith while the season of harvest is at hand. Draw near to God this moment, for you do not know what the next moment may bring.

The Danger of Delay
I've always been fascinated by Acts 17, which describes Paul's visit to Athens—a city with a thousand pagan gods—where he gave his powerful speech on Mars Hill at a place called the Areopagus, a popular spot in Athens where people of every imaginable kind would stand up and say their piece. The Areopagus was kind of like the Internet of Paul's day. Historians tell us that you could hardly move down the streets of Athens without bumping into someone selling idols.

When Paul got up to speak, he didn't give some store-bought, canned evangelistic sermon. Instead, he immediately revealed that he had made a quick but thorough study of Athens and the city's booming religious culture:

> Men of Athens! I see that in every way you are very religious. For as I walked around and looked carefully at your objects of worship, I even found an altar with this inscription: TO AN UNKNOWN GOD. Now what you worship as something unknown I am going to proclaim to you (Acts 17:22,23).

Paul was just getting started. To the residents of a city full of pagan idols and temples, he boldly said, "The God who made the world and everything in it is the Lord of heaven and earth and does not live in temples built by hands" (verse 24). Paul tried to explain the Christian message in a way the Athenians could understand. He even quoted some of the popular Athenian poets, using their words to illustrate the message of the gospel. Then he concluded by giving his hearers a straightforward invitation to accept Christ:

> In the past God overlooked such ignorance, but now he commands all people everywhere to repent. For he has set a day when he will judge the world with justice by the man he has appointed. He has given proof of this to all men by raising him from the dead (Acts 17:30,31).

Now it was up to his hearers to respond, and Luke, the author of Acts, tells us that they did so in three different ways. (By the way, I mentioned these three responses in chapter 5, but now we'll take a closer look.)

As usually happened when Paul preached, a few of his hearers believed. Luke doesn't give us a precise number of how many, but he does mention some of the better known individuals who became believers that day: "Among them was Dionysius, a member of the Areopagus, also a woman named Damaris, and a number of others" (verse 34).

There was also a group that had the opposite response. "Some of them sneered," Luke tells us, or as other translations express it, "some of them began to mock him" (verse 32). There will always be mockers in every crowd. They're here at Brownsville every night. I pray for them, but I try not to let them disturb me, and Paul didn't seem to be bothered by them too much, either. These people even get their own sentence in the New Testament. Jude, which is the little book right before Revelation, the last book in the Bible, tells us: "In the last times there will be scoffers who will follow their own ungodly desires" (Jude 18).

Luke tells us about a third group, and it's this group I want you to think about. Luke discusses this group only briefly with the following words: "Others said, 'We want to hear you again on this subject'" (verse 32). He tells us nothing about who these people were, or what they were thinking. Were these sincere seekers of God who really wanted to come back the next day and hear Paul say more? Were they people who had absolutely no interest in the things Paul was saying, but tried to look polite and friendly? Or were they procrastinators who were touched by what Paul said but wanted to forget about it for as long as possible? We'll never know. Luke couldn't see into their souls.

It didn't make any difference whether they were sincerely interested or thoroughly uninterested, because as the first verse of Acts 18 informs us, "After this, Paul left Athens and went to Corinth." It didn't make any difference what these people thought or wanted, because his speech that day was going to be their only opportunity to hear Paul deliver the gospel message. The next day, he was going to be on the road to the next city. Take heed to these words: The opportunity of a lifetime must be seized during the lifetime of the opportunity. As I write these words, perhaps you are standing at the very threshold of heaven. You are so close, but close doesn't count. The Lord is ready and willing to open the door and let you in. Unfortunately, these people missed their chance; don't miss yours.

The time of harvest had come, but these people did not respond. Paul was gone. Winter was on its way. The pumpkins had been thrashed by the hail and now lay stinking in the hot Alabama sun. My friend, learn this lesson: Don't hesitate.

Procrastination Station

There are a million and one reasons why people delay responding to God. Perhaps it would be helpful if we examined a few of the most notorious ones.

One of the all-time most popular reasons to delay is because religious people—who are often the instruments God uses to deliver His message—often seem pretty weird. Prophets like Jeremiah experienced this kind of disdain.

Another man of God who was thought weird by his contemporaries was Noah, the man God called to build an ark. I'll admit, building a big boat miles away from the nearest water isn't normal everyday behavior. It's even stranger when the guy building the boat starts loading it full of all kinds of animals. But as the book of Genesis tells us, "Noah did everything just as God had commanded him." God had warned Noah that a huge cataclysmic flood was coming. Noah believed Him and did what he was told.

WHY DO PEOPLE DELAY AND PROCRASTINATE? DON'T THEY REALIZE THAT LIFE IS FULL OF OPPORTUNITIES THAT ARE HERE FOR ONLY A SHORT TIME AND THEN PASS INTO ETERNITY, NEVER TO BE REPEATED AGAIN?

Unfortunately, we don't know how Noah's friends and neighbors reacted to the whole project. Perhaps they ridiculed him and threw rocks at him. Maybe they sat around in their lawn chairs, drinking, and laughing at him. Perhaps an enterprising neighbor even sold tickets and parking spaces to people interested in checking the scene out for themselves.

We do know that none of his neighbors joined Noah and his family on the ark. Some of them may have been planning to board at the last minute if it really looked like a flood was coming, but the Bible says the door was shut and sealed by God. Their window of opportunity had passed. Noah was on the ark, while they were in the dark.

Other people simply delay because they are sure they'll have plenty of opportunities to act on God's call tomorrow or the next day. That was the case with Larry, a friend I had known for years during my drug days. Larry was a master carpenter who could take a stack of lumber and turn it into a beautiful kitchen or bookcase. He was truly an incredibly talented artist.

Larry had heard about my conversion to Christ, my growth in God and my call to the ministry. I had talked to him once or twice since my conversion, but he showed little interest. There was a three-month period when I hadn't talked to Larry, and I was wondering how he was. Then my mom sent me a copy of the *Huntsville Times* newspaper. Right there before my eyes was an article about him. He had died of a drug overdose. This wonderful guy who was a talented artist and the son of a prominent Huntsville family was gone. Harvest time had come and gone.

Why do people delay and procrastinate? Don't they realize that life is full of opportunities that come only once and are here for only a short time, and then pass into eternity, never to be repeated again?

Have you ever heard the term "final exam"? It means this test is the last test you are going to take in a particular class. If you miss it, you fail it. If you snooze, you lose.

Have you ever heard the term "launch window"? This is a term NASA engineers use when they're getting ready to launch a space shuttle. The engineers calculate the trajectory of these big ships down to the tiniest degree and then select a target date for the best launch day. If that day comes and the weather suddenly turns bad for a few hours, the launch is canceled. Sometimes it can't be rescheduled for weeks.

Commercial airplanes also have windows of opportunity in which they must land and take off. If they miss their allotted time, that time is taken by another flight.

Sporting events are perhaps the best example of the danger of delay. Many sporting events are governed by the clock. You can make a great touchdown, but if it happens after the final buzzer has sounded, it doesn't count. You can make a great three-point basket, but if the time on the clock has expired, the points are worthless.

In March 1998, a high-powered tornado cut through northeast Georgia, causing destruction in five counties and killing 13 people. Surprisingly, none of the meteorologists who track such storms had been able to see this one coming. An article about the storm on CNN's website contained this frightening headline: "No chance for a warning."

COME HOME BEFORE DARK

I live out in rural Alabama with my wife and our three children. When Ryan, Shelby and Kelsey go out to play, they don't have to worry about busy streets with a lot of traffic. But even in the country, kids need to be cautious; they need to be on the lookout for things like snakes and spiders.

As a father, I am concerned about my kids, and I want to know where they are. So when it's afternoon, and our son Ryan wants to go out and play with some of his friends in the woods near our home, I look him in the eyes and tell him, "OK, son. Have fun. Be careful. And make sure you come home before dark." Around our house, the phrase "Come home before dark" has become a regular refrain.

I try not to be hypervigilant when Ryan is out playing, and I am fine as long as it's light outside. But when the sun begins to go down and afternoon starts blending into dusk, I get concerned.

If it's dark out and Ryan's not home, I find myself wondering where he is, what he's doing and whether or not he's all right. When it starts getting dark, he's supposed to realize it's time for him to hop on his bicycle or go-cart and ride home. He and I have had these conversations time after time. He needs to start heading home while it's still day and he can still see the road in front of him, the trees around him and the snakes in the brush.

Ryan is generally a pretty good kid, but like all kids, there are times when he isn't as wise as he should be. I can remember one of these times clearly in my mind. It was well past dusk—it was downright dark outside—and Ryan had not come home yet. I was edgy. I jumped on our four-wheeler and began searching our property while Jeri stayed by the phone. Every time the phone rang, she wondered if it was him calling from a neighbor's house.

Finally, Ryan did call. Jeri ran to the phone and picked up the receiver. She could hear his pleading voice on the other end, saying, "Mommy, it's dark outside. I can't see the path. Can you send Daddy to come get me?"

"Yes, son," she said. "He'll come get you."

I got in the car and went to pick up Ryan and his bike at a neighbor's house. He was glad to see me, though a little worried about what I might say. But I hugged him, told him I loved him and let him know how glad I was that he was safe.

In the few moments it took us to drive back home, I talked to Ryan about what we could learn from the day. "Son," I said, "I've told you to come home before dark."

"But Daddy, the time went by so quickly. We were having so much fun."

"I know. But next time, you need to do a better job at keeping track of the time. You need to plan ahead and not get caught out in the dark. Can you do that for me?"

"Okay, Dad," he said. "I'm sorry. I'll do better next time."

If you can understand a father's love for his son, you can also understand God's deep love and concern for us, His children. God doesn't want us to get lost. He wants us to come to Him before it gets dark.

Some of you reading this book right now are living in the twilight of time. The sun has already gone down. There may still be faint traces of light, but you can't see real well.

Jesus understood such a time as this, and He talked about it to His disciples: "As long as it is day, we must do the work of him who sent me. Night is coming, when no one can work" (John 9:4).

Paul understood such a time as this, too, even though he expressed it in a different way than I have here (Paul talked about the approaching day, not the coming darkness, but I think his point remains the same):

> The hour has come for you to wake up from your slumber, because our salvation is nearer now than when we first believed. The night is nearly over; the day is almost here. So let us put aside the deeds of darkness and put on the armor of light (Romans 13:11,12).

Elsewhere, Paul expressed the same idea:

> As God's fellow workers we urge you not to receive God's grace in vain. For he says,
>
> > "In the time of my favor I heard you,
> > and in the day of salvation I helped you."
>
> I tell you, now is the time of God's favor, now is the day of salvation (2 Corinthians 6:1,2).

The night is coming, my friend. There will come a day when you will no longer be able to find the time to do all the things you always wanted to do. It will be too late to call on God and grow in His grace. It will be too late to begin serving God as you had always meant to do, before the pressures and challenges of life tied you down. All your "should haves" and "would haves" will be for naught.

The harvest time will have passed, the winter will be upon you.

KEEP ON WALKING

When we first began following God,
we had high hopes.
Then doubts and difficulties set in.
But God is with us, and He is cheering us on
to keep on walking.

When I was a teenager, one of the things my friends and I loved to do was to swim in the Tennessee River. Just outside Huntsville, there was a stretch of the river about 300 yards wide. Above it was a huge suspension bridge that provided us with great front-row seats for watching each swimmer's progress.

I remember once, one of our friends decided to swim across that river. A half dozen of us ran up onto the bridge to watch. He got a really good start and was making great progress toward the halfway point. But then he started slowing down. Next he started treading water. By this time, the current had brought him to a spot right beneath where we were standing on the bridge, and we all began yelling and screaming, "You can do it! Keep on swimming, you're halfway there!"

But our friend panicked, turned around and started swimming

back to the shore where he had started. The strange thing—and the rest of us could see this very clearly from the bridge—was that going backwards was going to be just as difficult as continuing to go forward to the other shore. It seemed obvious to us that once our friend had made it to the middle of the river, the best thing to do was to keep swimming for the other side. After all, that was his goal.

Sometimes when I look at people and the way they live their lives, I think a lot of us are like that boy in the river, particularly when it comes to continuing on in our relationship with God. We have asked Jesus to come into our lives, and we have started walking with Him through the joys and sorrows of life. But then temptation comes or disappointment strikes or our courage leaves us, and suddenly we decide to stop, turn around and head back to the place from which we have come.

Maybe there have been times in your life when you've felt like turning back. Maybe you've been let down by a church, a pastor or a Christian friend. Or perhaps the struggles you face seem so insurmountable that going back looks easier. But some of us standing on the bridge wish you could see things from our perspective. Going back won't be any easier than carrying on with the journey. The currents are just as tough when you go backward as when you go forward.

In this final chapter, I'm going to encourage you to go the distance. Like my friends on the bridge, I'm crying out to you, "Keep on going, you're halfway there!" Remember, you're not alone, and with God's help you can do it. And hopefully, the pages that follow will give you some of the tips and encouragement you need to keep on walking.

NO OTHER DOCTRINE

One of the reasons people lose hope is that doubts and fears can squeeze out their faith in God. Unanswered or unresolved questions can have a corrosive effect on our beliefs and values. When our grip on God grows weak, errors and falsehoods can invade our souls and cloud our minds.

After his dramatic conversion to Christ, the apostle Paul spent the rest of his adult life traveling the globe and spreading the gospel. It wasn't as if Paul didn't have challenges. He constantly faced trials and tribulations that would make most of my problems look puny by comparison. But he stayed on course, or as he put it once, he ran the race God had set before him.

Things weren't nearly so good in some of the churches Paul established. In many of his letters to these churches, he constantly had to remind believers to avoid false doctrine and keep on walking in the truth of God. Listen to his command to Timothy, his disciple and helper:

> As I urged you when I went into Macedonia, stay there in Ephesus so that you may command certain men not to teach false doctrines any longer nor to devote themselves to myths and endless genealogies. These promote controversies rather than God's work—which is by faith (1 Timothy 1:3,4).

Or read these direct sentences from a letter to one church:

> I am astonished that you are so quickly deserting the one who called you by the grace of Christ and are turning to a different gospel—which is really no gospel at all. Evidently some people are throwing you into confusion and are trying to pervert the gospel of Christ. But even if we or an angel from heaven should preach a gospel other than the one we preached to you, let him be eternally condemned! As we have already said, so now I say again: If anybody is preaching to you a gospel other than what you accepted, let him be eternally condemned! (Galatians 1:6-9).

If Paul sounds a bit angry, that's because he is. The truth matters, my friend, and those who try to drag us away from the truth cause more danger and despair than they could ever imagine. They also risk the wrath of God.

All kinds of people toss around that word "truth." Perhaps it would be a good idea for us to explore what it means. Remember, my friend, this entire book is dedicated to helping you make it to heaven. Jesus said, "I am the way, and the truth, and the life; no one comes to the Father, but through Me" (John 14:6, *NASB*). It is vital for you to not only know the Truth, but to live according to the Truth.

WHAT IS TRUTH?

Pontius Pilate was interrogating Jesus in preparation for sentencing Him to death. Jesus made a bold statement to the Roman official: "For this reason I was born, and for this I came into the world, to testify to the truth. Everyone on the side of truth listens to me" (John 18:37). Pilate's response was this simple but profound question: "What is truth?"

Jesus is the Truth. The words of Scripture are truth. Everything else that claims to be truthful must be measured against the perfect measuring rod of the truth God has revealed to us. That goes for articles in the daily newspaper as well as sermons by me or any other preacher.

Sometimes the Bible doesn't summarize things as clearly as people would like, so over the centuries Christian believers have written a series of creeds—or faith statements—designed to sum up the foundational truths the Bible teaches. One of the oldest and most trustworthy of these statements is the Apostles' Creed. Perhaps you have read it or heard it recited in church:

I believe in God the Father Almighty, maker of heaven
and earth;
And in Jesus Christ His only Son our Lord:
Who was conceived by the Holy Spirit,
Born of the Virgin Mary,
Suffered under Pontius Pilate,
Was crucified, dead, and buried;

He descended into hell;
The third day He rose from the dead;
He ascended into heaven,
And sits at the right hand of God the Father Almighty;
From whence He shall come to judge the living and the dead.
I believe in the Holy Spirit; the Holy Christian Church,
The communion of saints, the forgiveness of sins,
the resurrection of the body, and the life everlasting.
Amen.

There you have it. In 109 words, the Apostles' Creed gives us the best summary of Christian teaching that has ever been written. Each word and phrase is an expression of foundational biblical truths. You would do well to make a copy of this creed so you can study it, memorize it and meditate on its truth.

Some people today still ask Pilate's question, "What is truth?" Part of the reason they do so is because it seems that there are so many different churches in the world, and that these churches seem to disagree with each other about what is true. Sometimes, a pastor from one church may even have bad things to say about another pastor from another church.

This kind of disunity grieves God deeply, but should it cause us confusion? I don't think so.

VARIATIONS ON A THEME

There are hundreds of Christian denominations in the world. Among the Protestant denominations there are dozens of varieties of Baptists, Methodists, Lutherans and Presbyterians. As crazy as this may seem, the basic creeds of these denominations agree on just about all major issues.

We could devote hundreds of pages to this subject, but let me try to deal with it in just a few paragraphs. Below are summaries of what the creeds of some of the world's largest Christian groups say about two fundamental issues: Jesus and salvation. Look at these creeds and see if you can detect any significant differences in doctrine.

Lutheran
Jesus is the Son of God and the sacrifice offered for the forgiveness of sins on the cross. Man is forgiven by a Holy Spirit-empowered action of turning from sin directly to God.

Presbyterian
Jesus is the Son of God, and He holds sovereignty in salvation. There is no one else who can offer salvation to the soul. Man is a sinner saved by accepting God's irresistible grace offered in Jesus Christ.

Methodist
Jesus is the Son of God and Redeemer of mankind through His blood. Man is a sinner naturally, and needs conversion and repentance to be saved.

Episcopal
Jesus is the Son of God, conceived by the Holy Spirit and given birth by the virgin Mary. He was crucified and was buried and then rose again for the redemption of sinners. Faith in Jesus Christ is the only way to have salvation from sin.

Assemblies of God
Jesus is the only Son of God, second member of the Trinity, who was born of a virgin, died on the cross for redemption and was raised again after three days for justification of the converted. All men are sinners and are saved by grace through faith in Jesus Christ, demonstrated by repentance of sin.

I could go on, but do you get the picture? In classical music, composers wrote compositions they called "Theme and Variations." For example, Bach would take a piece of music such as "God Save the

Queen" as a theme. Then he would devise a series of variations on that theme. Some variations were in a fast pace and a major key, others in a slow pace and a minor key. But even though all these variations sounded different, you could hear the theme coming through clear as a bell. That's the way it is with the denominations and their creeds. Each group expresses the same foundational truths in its own way.

I'm not saying there are no differences in the ways Pentecostals and Episcopalians dress, worship or build churches. There are plenty of human differences in all of these denominations, and that's exactly what they are: human differences. But if you look at their core beliefs and doctrines, there is a surprising uniformity. This is why people from all denominations attend our Awake America crusades throughout America. Most denominations agree on the important issues, and anyone who claims that different churches preach different gospels is either confused or is intentionally trying to pull a choir robe over your eyes!

Mark Twain, who was one of the best American-born writers to ever pick up a pen, once said something that was very insightful. I'm paraphrasing it here, but what he said went something like this: It's not the things in the Bible I don't understand that bother me. It's the things I do understand that bother me!

The Bible is a big, complex book. It contains 66 books, 1,189 chapters and 31,173 verses. Certainly there are some things in the Bible that are open for debate. For example, believers have been known to argue over what I call non-issues, like whether Paul was riding a horse or a donkey when he was visited by Jesus on his way to Damascus. I find debates of this nature mildly interesting, but to me the important thing is that Jesus visited Paul, a man who had formerly been the foremost persecutor of Christ's followers, and transformed him into the Church's foremost evangelist. To me, that's the important thing, and I believe that when it comes to important things, the Bible is amazingly clear and straightforward.

For years, a man named Peter Marshall was the chaplain of the United States Senate. (The Senate still has a chaplain, folks, and

Congress doesn't seem to feel that it's a violation of the separation of church and state!) Marshall published some of his prayers, and the following prayer says much about the wide gulf that often separates what we say from what we believe:

> Forgive us, Lord Jesus, for doing the things that make us uncomfortable and guilty when we pray. We say that we believe in God, yet we doubt all your promises. We say that in God we trust, yet we worry and try to manage our own affairs. We say that we love you, O Lord, but we don't obey you. We believe that you have the answer to all our problems, but we don't even talk to you about them. Forgive us, Lord Jesus, for lack of faith and the willful pride that ignores the way, the truth and the life.[1]

As Marshall so powerfully shows, for most of us, the question isn't, What is truth? Rather, for us, the question is, What are we going to do about the truth?

CREEDS OF THE UNCOMMITTED

The truth of God is clear. Now God demands our response. Those who swear total allegiance to the truth of God are the committed. These people are dedicated, obligated and actively involved in living out the Christian faith.

But there is another group. I call them the uncommitted. They are indifferent, hesitant, unresolved, apathetic and unfaithful. These people are too wishy-washy to develop their own creed, so I have done it for them. I call it "The Creed of the Uncommitted." Here are its cardinal doctrines:

Thou shalt worship other idols before God
Sure, God told us in the Ten Commandments to have no other idols before Him, but that doesn't make any difference to the uncommit-

ted. In fact, they let almost anything take the place of Christ.

For many adults, it's the demands of a job or career that often take first place in their lives. For young people, it may be a boyfriend or girlfriend who occupies every waking and dreaming moment. Parents can make idols out of their kids. Citizens can make idols out of their political views, pet issues and favorite can-

> GOD'S TRUTH STANDS AS A ROCK IN THE SHIFTING TIDES OF OUR TIME, A TALL PILLAR AMID THE BLOWING SANDS OF CHAOS AND CHANGE. WE DO NOT NEED TO CHANGE GOD'S TRUTH; RATHER, WE NEED TO LET GOD'S TRUTH TRANSFORM US.

didates. And if all of these fail, there are always riches and pleasure, which have been among humanity's most prized idols from the beginning of time.

In the long run, it doesn't make that much difference to the uncommitted which specific idol you choose, just as long as you worship it above and before God.

Thou shalt modify the Word of God

The argument of the uncommitted goes like this: Life is full of flux and change, so why shouldn't Christianity change right along with it? Those biblical injunctions against adultery and homosexuality? They sound puritanical, so let's delete them. Those commandments against stealing and lying? They limit our lifestyle options, so let's edit them out.

Friend, I know a few things about editing. After this book was turned into the publisher, an editor suggested many ways it could be improved. Some concepts could be made clearer, some passages cleaner and simpler. I have no problem with that. I'm open to correction. But God's Word doesn't need any editing or correction. The Word is true, no matter how uncomfortable it makes us feel or how unfashionable some of its doctrines may seem to some people.

Life is full of change, but God's truth isn't. It stands as a rock in the shifting tides of our time, a tall pillar amid the blowing sands of chaos and change. We do not need to change God's truth; rather, we need to let God's truth transform us.

Thou shalt be unreliable and self-centered

God wants servants who can be called on to stand up for righteousness and truth. The uncommitted don't stand for much of anything. In fact, they'd rather sit, if you don't mind.

Is there a prayer meeting at church? The uncommitted would rather watch ESPN or HBO. Is there a young person at church who needs a mentor, an old person who needs comfort, a married couple who needs counseling? Sorry, but the uncommitted have their own problems to deal with. Is there an important project that requires skill and reliability? Don't bother with the uncommitted. They have plenty of talent and skill, but don't ask them to share any of it with you or the church.

Thou shalt assume that God will forgive and forget

If there's one doctrine the uncommitted believe in, it is that God is love. In fact, these people are banking on the hope that God forgives and forgets all, because they have an awful lot to be forgiven. As for those verses in the Bible that talk about God being a holy and righteous judge? Must be a mistranslation, they say. Our God would never be so narrow-minded.

God is not narrow-minded, my friend, but Christianity is narrow. In fact, sometimes it's so narrow that you can feel it rubbing your shoulders as you walk in it. Listen to these words of Jesus:

"Enter through the narrow gate. For wide is the gate and broad is the road that leads to destruction, and many enter through it. But small is the gate and narrow the road that leads to life, and only a few find it" (Matthew 7:13,14).

According to Solomon, we should avoid the uncommitted: "Like a bad tooth or a lame foot is reliance on the unfaithful in times of trouble" (Proverbs 25:19). Instead, we should cast ourselves upon the reliable truth of God.

Radically Committed to the Truth

The word "radical" means different things to different people. In the 1960s, it often referred to long-haired anti-establishment types who were involved in protesting the war in Vietnam or thumbing their noses at "plastic" America. I was part of this group during my hippie days. In the 1990s, it sometimes referred to short-haired Republican types involved in protesting at abortion clinics or thumbing their noses at Hollywood.

But radical doesn't refer to people who are on either the left or the right, it refers to people who find the truth at the bottom of things. Larry Tomczak is a bold minister who teaches at the Brownsville Revival School of Ministry. In his book *Divine Appointments*, Larry talks about what it means to be radical:

A genuine disciple of Jesus Christ must be radical. Not radical in the political sense but in the sense of the Latin word it comes from: *radix*, or root. Christians are people who have been changed "from the root." This speaks of an inner transformation so radical that it cannot help but result in changed behavior. This is the kind of change John the Baptist was looking for when he told his hearers to "produce fruit in keeping with repentance" (Matthew 3:8). Jesus meant what He said: "Any of you who does not give up everything he has cannot be my disciple" (Luke 14:33). "Not everyone who says to me, 'Lord, Lord,' will enter the kingdom of heaven, but only he who does the will of my Father who is in heaven" (Matthew 7:21).[2]

Are you a radical disciple, or are you only a passive observer? Is your relationship to God a flame that burns within you or a big wet blanket that extinguishes the fire? Are you following Jesus, the compassionate Savior who is also a righteous judge, or do you follow whoever comes along and says something interesting? Are you willing to take a stand for something, or are you ready to stand for just about anything?

Martin Luther was a Roman Catholic who began reading his Bible more seriously, believing what it said and applying it with his life. He never planned on starting the Protestant Reformation, but his ideas—which were based on the truths of Scripture—propelled this powerful movement. As he once said:

> Far from being alarmed, it gives me great joy to see that the gospel is now, as in former times, a cause of trouble and discord. This is the characteristic and the destiny of the Word of God. "I come not to send peace, but a sword," said Jesus Christ [Matthew 10:34].[3]

When God revealed His truth to humanity, He didn't send us a Hallmark card with a smiley face on the front. He sent us a tough message that invades our souls and transforms our lives. I pray that you will allow God to use His truth to transform you.

YOU AND THE TRUTH

We've come to the end of this book. Over the past 12 chapters we've discussed many things, and perhaps you're feeling overwhelmed or confused. Let me close by asking one simple, straightforward question: What are you going to do about God and everything He has revealed to you?

Remember, 78 percent of North Americans believe they have an excellent or good chance of making it to heaven. Friend, you don't need to chance it. You can be certain.

Someone told me years ago that the truest test of a person's soul happens when that person is all alone and no one else is watching. When people are at work or at church, they often play-act in ways that are designed to impress others. They try to look more intelligent or more together than they really are so that people will like them and think highly of them.

As understandable as such acting is, the real truth of who you are and what you believe can best be found in solitude. Who are you when no one else is around for you to impress? What is the true nature of your character when you aren't being distracted by the crush of the crowd?

As you sit there reading these final words, I pray that you will choose to follow Jesus Christ, and that you will do so with all your heart.

Remember that becoming a true Christian involves repentance. Once you've repented of your sin, you make a conscious decision to stop sinning. Sin will always separate you from God. And it causes a barrier between you and heaven.

Don't put it off. Pray and ask Jesus Christ to forgive you, wash your sins away, and make you a new person. By making this decision now, you will experience what millions around the world are enjoying—true peace and fellowship with God. And when your life comes to an end and you find yourself standing at heaven's door, don't bother to knock. You're family. Come on in.

God bless you.

Notes

1. Peter Marshall, 81st Congress, 1st Session, Senate Document No. 86, Washington, D.C.: U.S. Government Printing Office, 1949.
2. Larry Tomczak, *Divine Appointments* (Ann Arbor, Mich.: Servant Publications, 1986), p. 152.
3. Thomas Sefton Rivington, *The Story of Martin Luther's Life* (Simpkin, Marshall, Hamilton, Kent & Co., n.d.), p. 317.

S T E P H E N   H I L L

TEN MOST

WANTED

Can You Think of 10 People You Want Saved?

One of the greatest obstacles to winning souls is fear. People, for the most part, don't witness because they are afraid of not knowing what to say or how to say it. The "Ten Most Wanted" home crusade project takes that obstacle out of the way by providing you with resources which will equip and empower you for effective soul winning.

Each Packet contains a clear and penetrating message from Stephen Hill, filmed at an Awake America crusade. God is using these messages to break hard hearts and call many to repentance. We are already receiving reports of entire families falling to their knees together in the living room, accepting Jesus as Savior through one of these messages! The tape concludes with a special one-on-one call to repentance from Steve to your loved ones.

To oder a copy of this dynamic video, or more information about Together in the Harvest Ministries, Inc. , write to:

Together in the Harvest Ministries, Inc.

P. O. Box 2090
Foley, Alabama 36536

Or visit our website at:

You also receive a Prayer Covenant Card, ten Invitation Cards, ten copies of Steve's testimony book Stone Cold Heart, and follow-up materials. The extraordinary potential of this program begins with prayer. Ask God to help you identify ten people you know that need Him most. As you begin praying for their salvation on a daily basis, write and request your "Ten Most Wanted" packet!

w w w . s t e v e h i l l . o r g